New Testament Commentary by a Mathematician

Victor Porton

Copyright © 2015 Victor Porton

Table of Contents

Preface

Gospel about one's own validity

Gospel: Life, death, and resurrection

Christ and God

Jesus' life on Earth

Salvation

Reincarnation

Interpretation of Bible

Prosperity Gospel

Miscellaneous

Apocalypse

Further readings

Chapter 1 Preface

In this book I am going to tell you my thoughts on the New Testament, so you will know the same mysteries as me.

Throughout, I will note all interesting or important things I have discovered in the New Testament that are not trivial. In other words, things that are not readily evident without engaging in a scrutinized study.

I lay no claim to infallibility, for to do so would be presumptuous. Rather, what is written is the personal opinion of Victor Porton. I am a man and may err.

Bible quotes are taken from the World English Bible unless otherwise specified.

Unlike some other Bible commentaries, this book is grouped by topics rather than the order of verses.

If you have never taken the time to read the New Testament in its entirety, I highly recommend you read it prior to continuing on with this book.

Although there are a large variety of translations available, I recommend World English Bible.

Chapter 2 Gospel about one's own validity

Throughout this work I will use the titles *Gospel* and *New Testament* interchangeably to refer to the 27 books that comprise the canon of scripture that was finished a little less than 2,000 years ago. Using the Gospel, I will show that it approves its own validity as God's word.

Certainly we cannot simply conclude that the Gospel is true just because it claims to be true. If that were so, then any number of ancient texts from various cultures would have an equally valid claim. However, we can infer something from the fact that the Gospel asserts its own validity: namely that it cannot be half-true. If the Gospel is something only near to the truth, then its assertion to be errorless and thus God's word should make us believe that it truly is errorless. By contrast, if it were not near to the truth, it would be made even farther from the truth by its own assertion of divine authorship while containing untruths.

"Heaven and earth will pass away, but my words will not pass away." (Mt. 24:35)

"Heaven and earth will pass away, but my words will not pass away." (Mrk. 13:31)

"Heaven and earth will pass away, but my words will by no means pass away." (Luk. 21:33)

"But the Counselor, the Holy Spirit, whom the Father will send in my name, he will teach you all things, and will remind you of all that I said to you." (Jn. 14:26)

As they were reminded by the Holy Spirit, the authors of the Gospels described the words of Jesus exactly and without errors.

"I tell the truth in Christ. I am not lying, my conscience testifying with me in the Holy Spirit." (Rom. 9:1)

Peter equates Paul's letters with former (Old Testament) scriptures: (2Pet. 3:16) **"as also in all of his letters, speaking in them of these things. In those are some things hard to be understood,**

which the ignorant and unsettled twist, as they also do to the other Scriptures, to their own destruction."

Thus you are faced with a stark choice: Believe the Gospel accounts in their entirety or reject them as nothing more than an historical myth.

Gospel about validity of Old Testament

If one truly believes what is recorded in the Gospel, this belief also necessitates a belief in the accounts recorded in the Old Testament. The reason being, oftentimes the New Testament refers to the Old Testament as a proof text for many of its claims. Here are some examples:

"For most assuredly, I tell you, until heaven and earth pass away, not even one smallest letter or one tiny pen stroke shall in any way pass away from the law, until all things are accomplished." (Mt. 5:18)

"But it is easier for heaven and earth to pass away, than for one tiny stroke of a pen in the law to fall." (Luk. 16:17)

"The book of the generation of Jesus Christ, the son of David, the son of Abraham. ..." (Mt. 1)

"... for thus it is written through the prophet..." (Mt. 2:5)

"that it might be fulfilled which was spoken by the Lord through the prophet." (Mt. 2:15)

See also Mt. 12:17; Mt. 3:3; 4:7; 4:14-16; 8:17; 13:14; 13:35; 15:7-8; 21:4-5; 21:42; 22:32; 22:43-44; 27:9-10; Mrk. 1:2-3; Mrk. 7:6-7; 12:10-11; 12:36; 14:27; Luk. 1:55; 1:70; 2:23; 3:4-6; Luk. 7:27

"He said to them, 'This is what I told you, while I was still with you, that all things which are written in the law of Moses, the prophets, and the psalms, concerning me must be fulfilled.'" (Luk. 24:44)

cf. Jn. 1:23; Jn. 12:14-15; Jn. 12:38-41; 15:25; 19:24; 19:28; 19:36-37; Act. 2:16-21; 2:25-28; 4:25-

26; 7:43; 7:48-50; Rom. 1:2; 3:4; 3:10-18; 4:3; 4:17; 9:25-29; 9:33; 10:5; 10:15; 10:19-21; 11:8-11; 11:26; 14:11; 15:9-12; 15:21; 1Cor. 1:19; 2:9; 9:9; 15:3-4; 1Tim. 5:18

"**Every writing inspired by God is profitable for teaching, for reproof, for correction, and for instruction which is in righteousness.**" (2Tim. 3:16)

Cf. Heb. 8:8; 10:16; 10:30; 1Pet. 2:6-8, 2Pet. 3:2

Chapter 3 Gospel: Life, death, and resurrection

Because the New Testament is God's word, there are no contradictions (nor any other errors) in it.

That being said, there are a significant number of seeming contradictions throughout the New Testament. For instance, it records how Christ died, yet goes on to proclaim He is alive and will never die again. To understand this dichotomy, which is one of the foundational elements of the Christian faith, we need the God's word resolution of this as well as other supposed contradictions. The resolution is that Christ resurrected. The scripture refers to Jesus as the firstborn from the dead, meaning he is the first person who will ever die that will never die a second time. Jesus established the pattern where he lived, died then lived again, never to die.

"In the beginning was the Word, and the Word was with God, and the Word was God. The same was in the beginning with God." (Jn. 1:1-2)

This passage plainly refers to Jesus Christ, who St. John identified by the use of the word "logos," (literally "word" in the English language) the deity of ancient Greek philosophers. Although I am not quite certain, I think this can also be applied to any part of God's word, including the Gospel. Thus I conclude that the Gospel should follow the same pattern as Christ himself: the Gospel lives, dies, and is resurrected.

This means that our first interpretation of a passage lives for a period of time, but then dies when we realize that our first understanding was wrong. Then, after a period of time, it should resurrect! When this occurs it means that our first understanding was correct, it just was not compatible with our overall philosophy.

I submit that the New Testament is inherently filled with things which look like contradictions when in reality, all it is doing is following this life-death-resurrection pattern, which is nothing more than seemingly improbable combinations of things. In human logic, life is not compatible with death, but the

Gospel teaches about resurrection, that is, merging two seemingly incompatible things (life and death) together.

You should try to always follow this life-death-resurrection pattern when interpreting the Gospel, otherwise you too will easily fall into contradictions. However, I must confess that I have not always followed this pattern, because my knowledge of the Bible is not perfect.

One may reasonably ask the question: If a passage of the Gospel dies, and then resurrects, can it ever die again? No, it can't be: "**knowing that Christ, being raised from the dead, dies no more. Death no more has dominion over him!**" (Rom. 6:9) This means we don't need to overload our mind with repeated deaths and resurrections again in our understanding of the Gospel. So the pattern life-death-resurrection in our understanding of the Gospel is simple enough for us to understand. (There is only three stages, not an infinite sequence of repeated deaths and resurrections.)

Prosperity Gospel as an example

Some Christian denominations, primarily Charismatics, believe in the Prosperity doctrine or Prosperity Gospel. Other denominations, both evangelical and liberal, such as Methodists or Baptists, reject this teaching and even say that it is a heresy.

For those who may be unaware of what this teaching is; the *Prosperity Gospel* is the belief that faith, when combined with following certain commandments, primarily those involving giving money to God's work or those who need it, results in making the giver prosperous, not only in heaven but also in this world. This prosperity takes the form or earthly wealth and influence.

Proponents of this doctrine point to Bible verses, such as the well-known "blessing of Abraham" (who was a rich man by the standards of his day). Likewise, opponents quote other Bible verses to support their case.

Provided our faith is correct, I do not doubt that with God's help we can obtain everything we request. **"Or do you think that I couldn't ask my Father, and he would even now send me more than twelve legions of angels?"** (Mt. 26:53); **"... how much more will your Father who is in heaven give good things to those who ask him"** (Mt. 7:11); **"All things, whatever you ask in prayer, believing, you will receive."** (Mt. 21:22); **"Therefore I tell you, all things whatever you pray and ask for, believe that you receive them, and you shall have them."** (Mrk. 11:24); **"Whatever you will ask in my name, that will I do, that the Father may be glorified in the Son. If you will ask anything in my name, I will do it."** (Jn. 14:13); **"If you remain in me, and my words remain in you, you will ask whatever you desire, and it will be done for you."** (Jn. 15:7); **"... that whatever you will ask of the Father in my name, he may give it to you."** (Jn. 15:16); **"... Most assuredly I tell you, whatever you may ask of the Father in my name, he will give it to you."** (John 16:23)

During the first few years after my conversion to Christ I lived in extreme poverty. Things were so bad I was afraid I would die of hunger. Even later when I believed the Prosperity doctrine and was asking God to give me money, I wasn't receiving the promised blessings. I was in conflict with everybody, because I was constantly quarreling about the Bible with anyone who would listen. The verses are plain in their promises, so if they were not evident in my life the problem is not the bible, rather my faith was wrong. (Or do you think having the right faith leads to a meaningless death by starvation?) I could be not a preacher, because if I preached in a church, all of my sermons would be "how to behave in such a way as to conflict with everyone and die of hunger." I was living a life of following a self-contradictory doctrine. It was all about me: "**For let that man not think that he will receive anything from the Lord. He is a double-minded man, unstable in all his ways.**" (James 1:7-8)

Now I have no doubt that if a person's faith is correct and they pray for money then God will answer.

The question is should we ask God to give us large sums of money? Should we practice the commandments of prosperity for the sake of prosperity?

It looks like that Gospel indicates that the answer is a resounding **no!** "**But having food and clothing, we will be content with that. But those who are determined to be rich fall into a temptation and a snare and many foolish and harmful lusts, such as drown men in ruin and destruction.**" (1Tim. 6:8-9)

This verse is the *death* of the Prosperity doctrine.

But remember, in the Gospel death is followed by a resurrection! "**Count it all joy, my brothers, when you fall into various temptations, knowing that the testing of your faith produces endurance. Let endurance have its perfect work, that you may be perfect and complete, lacking in nothing.**" (Jam. 1:2-4) In this passage, "various" includes the temptation of richness. So when God gives us richness we should accept it with great joy. We should lack in nothing (be rich) according to the above Bible quote. Also, "**Blessed is the man who endures temptation, for when he has been approved, he will receive the crown of life, which the Lord promised to those who love him.**" (Jam. 1:12)

"**But let the brother in humble circumstances glory in his high position; and the rich, in that he is made humble, because like the flower in the grass, he will pass away**" (Jam. 1:9-10). This is the reverse of what we thought.

Those who have riches should understand that they are tempted more than those who have little or nothing. "**Come now, you rich, weep and howl for your miseries that are coming on you.**" (Jam. 5:1)

One may ask: Why does the author believe that we should come into temptations? The answer is found in James 1:2-4 quoted above. I will say more about going through temptations later in this book.

See chapter Chapter 9 for more on the Prosperity Gospel.

Chapter 4 Christ and God
Foreword

Obtaining a human understanding of God is difficult. At times it seems that a human can only reason about God through the use of analogies.

Many different analogies for God have been proposed to help explain God. Some of them are quite helpful while others are completely pointless.

The first analogy which comes to mind concerns a comparison of God to a human being. This is natural for Abrahamic religions as it states "**God said, "Let us make man in our image, after our likeness"** (Ge. 1:26).

The comparison of God with a man is a good analogy, but it lacks a proper explanation of Holy Trinity. It was proposed that the trinity is similar to a mentally disordered person having three personalities, but in my opinion this analogy is entirely pointless.

I propose a different analogy to describe God. God is similar to a *civilization*. To be sure, this is indeed a very deep analogy. In this analogy there is even a place for analogies of Christ, which is similar to a "contact" of a civilization that is to a less advanced civilization making *contact* with a more advanced one or to contact between parts of an advanced civilization and by comparing the Holy Spirit to the *technology* of a civilization. This is not to suggest we are able to come to a knowledge of the existence and properties of Christ and the Holy Spirit based solely on philosophical grounds without the help of the Bible; but nevertheless Christ and Holy Spirit (and therefore the Holy Trinity) have a natural place in this philosophy.

With this theology there is a good fit for mankind's purpose and position in the universe as being unlimitedly developed with God's help.

As such, I consider a *civilization* to be the best known analogy for studying God.

Let us examine some similarities and differences between a civilization and God.

Note that when speaking about civilizations and outside contact, I will make not mention of aliens from outer space, because we are mostly interested in the common properties of civilizations and God, not in how a civilization may be split into parts. "**For there is no partiality with God**" (Rom. 2:11). This verse indicates that analyzing God through the use of an analogy of something split into parts may be not effective.

God as a civilization

I am using the word *universe* to refer to the totality of physical reality. In other words, the universe consists of anything that physically exists. This would include galaxies, stars, atoms, electrons, everything. I refer not only to the visible part of universe which astronomers can see, but the entire universe including hidden dimensions. Astronomers have long debated the size of the universe. The leading theory in vogue is that the universe is finite. However, I believe the universe is infinite because (as I demonstrate below) an infinite Christ lives inside the universe.

Consider the ramifications of an infinite Universe. Within it various civilizations have reached different levels of development.

Because the Universe is infinite, it is natural to assume the existence of civilizations at all possible levels of development. Extending this reasoning, we may conclude that there exist civilizations of infinitely high level of development.

The natural question arises, does there exist several different civilizations at this infinite level of development or is there only one united civilization at the infinite level of development. If we call a civilization with this infinite level of development *god*, this question gets reformulated: whether there are several different gods or one god? (More exactly, an infinitely developed civilization in the Universe is a representation of God, not God Himself. I will consider this below.)

Well, what do we mean when we say "there exists just one civilization possessing an infinite level of development"? We could split a civilization into multiple parts and call them different civilizations. So the key to this question is not *quantity* but *unity*. By this I mean that the question of whether there is only one god should be reformulated: are all the entities with this infinite level of development *united* with each other? Do they share one common business? Are they in peace with each other? Some translators of the Bible prefer to say "God is united" instead of "There is one God."

In other words, when we say "there is one god" what we really mean is that all infinitely developed civilizations coincide. What do I mean when I say *coincide*? This is a hard question and I am not able to offer a precise definition. If we consider it from the civilizational viewpoint, this would be a social relation and social relations are difficult to be defined exactly. I'm going to attempt to describe some of these properties. First, all gods are at peace with each other. If we had two infinitely developed civilizations at war with each other, this would mean there are two different gods. The second aspect of God's unity is that He is personal. This means He has a united opinion and makes united decisions.

According to the doctrine of Holy Trinity God has not one, but three persons.

In several key aspects God differs from what we call a civilization. For example, a civilization has a definitive time and place where it first began. Rome supposedly began when Romulus killed his brother Remus and founded the city on the Palatine Hill. The civilization that formed the United States had its beginning with the American Revolution. However, God is eternal. Despite these differences I will compare God with a civilization throughout the rest of this chapter.

Thus I conclude that God is similar to a highly developed civilization, yet He is highly united, personal, eternal, and infinite.

So I submit to you the following:

Postulate: The Universe is infinite.

Postulate: God exists.

Postulate: God is one or united.

Postulate: God is personal.

Christ

If God is a civilization then Christ is its contact.

Christ is electromagnetic energy

Civilizations primarily engage in communication through the use of electromagnetic waves such as radio or television signals.

Since Christ is the mediator between God and man, it is natural to think of Christ as being similar to electromagnetic waves.

In fact, the Bible teaches that Christ is all of the electromagnetic waves throughout the Universe.

"**… Jesus spoke to them, saying, 'I am the light of the world…;**" (Jn. 8:12)

"**While I am in the world, I am the light of the world.**" (Jn. 9:5)

"**I have come as a light into the world…**" (Jn. 12:46)

Waves in the electromagnetic spectrum are a picture of both Christ's incarnation in the Universe (Jn. 9:5; Jn. 12:46) as well as a full description of Christ (Jn. 8:12).

I understand this as meaning that electromagnetic waves of the Universe are a complete characterization of Christ. But note that Christ reaches outside of the Universe. He is only electromagnetic energy or something like it while He is in the world (Universe).

A curious reader may doubt my interpretation of Matthew 5:14, "**You are the light of the world,**" and Ephesians 5:8 "**For you were once darkness, but are now light in the Lord…**" Are the ones Jesus is speaking to in these passages also electromagnetic waves of the Universe? Indeed they are.

"**… made us sit together in heavenly places in Christ Jesus.**" (Eph. 2:6)

The word "sit" is in the Aorist tense (a Greek grammatical form) that is in perfect past time. This means we are already in the heavens. This may seem counter-intuitive because we do not feel like we are in the heavens. I conclude that we currently exist in the heavens as electromagnetic waves. It can be said that we, as one body, form Christ (thus Christ may be considered as an organization or a collective). But Christ is Christ only without partiality. We are part of the universe's electromagnetic waves with partiality because every one of us is a part of the electromagnetic waves of the heavens.

How can we, being people, also be electromagnetic waves in the heaven? I understand this as being the existence of one-to-one correspondence between the structure of the electromagnetic waves in the heavens and us living on earth. I think the same applies to Christ's human nature. In the body of a man, Jesus mapped the structure of the light of the Universe. It is hard to believe and may seem absurd, but this what the Gospel requires us to believe. I continue to wonder what may be the reason for this one-to-one correspondence.

With Christ being the electromagnetic waves of the universe it then logically follows that the universe must be infinite because Christ is infinite. Thus the universe contains more than just the visible portion which is known to be finite.

Christ is also called logos (word) in the Bible because He is the Word of God (in the form of electromagnetic waves).

Wisdom and truth

Postulate: The knowledge of a highly developed civilization will more than likely be in the form of the electromagnetic waves.

In other words, Christ is God's wisdom.

"Christ is ... the wisdom of God." (1Cor. 1:24)

This means just two simple things:

- The word of God is wise.

- God has imparted all His wisdom in His word;

that is Christ is the entirety of the wisdom of God, not just parts (that exist in various forms and locations) of full wisdom. That Christ is the full content of God is also declared in the following verses.

"In the beginning was the Word, and the Word was with God, and the Word was God. The same was in the beginning with God. All things were made through him. Without him was not anything made that has been made." (Jn. 1:1-3)

"He was in the world, and the world was made through him, and the world didn't recognize him." (Jn. 1:10)

"… who created all things through Jesus Christ." (Eph. 3:9)

Because God is infinitely developed, His wisdom (knowledge) not only contains all truths, it is nothing but truth and contains no error. In other words, Christ is the logical truth. When Jesus speaks on a subject, it is the final word on it. He never has to go back and make corrections when "new evidence comes to light."

"Jesus said to him, 'I am the way, the truth, and the life.'" (Jn. 14:6)

"… Your word is truth." (Jn. 17:17)

I mentioned above that an infinite developed civilization is God, but that is actually not quite so. In Christianity this infinitely developed civilization in the Universe is called *Christ*. I will argue below that Christ is God, but only conditionally.

Peace

Which possible forms can a civilization take? It may be a peace treaty union.

Existence of one God may be understood as being the same as having complete peace between its parts. I said earlier that we are not able to precisely define the unity of God; but it is conceivable that this unity is the same as "peace in all aspects." The unity consists of the interchange of information ("contact") that is Christ.

A central concept in the issue of inter-civilization and intra-civilizational relations is *peace*.

According to the Bible, Christ is peace. I think this is equivalent to saying that Christ is the unity of God.

"**But now in Christ Jesus you who once were far off are made near in the blood of Christ. For he is our peace, who made both one, and broke down the middle wall of partition, having abolished in the flesh the hostility, the law of commandments contained in ordinances, that he might create in himself one new man of the two, making peace; and might reconcile them both in one body to God through the cross, having killed the hostility thereby. He came and preached peace to you who were far off and to those who were near. For through him we both have our access in one Spirit to the Father. So then you are no longer strangers and foreigners, but you are fellow citizens with the saints, and of the household of God.**" (Eph. 2:13-19)

This means that Christ is far more than just the peace union for the entire Universe; He is the peace with God.

Peace is great in the sense that there is no easy way to prevent war. The measures necessary to prevent war are great. Christ is the set of measures taken (on the heavens) to prevent war. To prevent war it is necessary something as great as Christ. Thus it can be said that Christ is the prevention of war or absence of war.

A paradoxical outcome of this attribute is that a seemingly little thing such as the absence of war needs to be as great as Christ.

It can be compared to reading a newspaper headline "Peace is established, war is abolished". That would be a very great headline.

"He said to them, 'But who do you say that I am?' Peter answered, 'The Christ of God." (Luk. 9:20)

This means that Christ is the contact of God, the means through which God communicates with Himself. Christ lives by the Father; and the Father also lives by Christ. Thus, Christ is essential for the Father's existence.

"Don't you believe that I am in the Father, and the Father in me? ... Believe me that I am in the Father, and the Father in me." (Jn. 14:10-11)

(Alternatively translated "I exist by the Father, and the Father exists by me"). Also Jn. 17:21.

Peace and wisdom are related: *Wisdom is internal peace.* When neurons are in a state of peace with each other, our brain would be cleverer than any brain! The peace of God is above (that is, more clever than) any mind ("surpasses all understanding")

"The peace of God, which surpasses all understanding, will guard your hearts and your thoughts in Christ Jesus." (Phil. 4:7)

Note however:

"'Don't think that I came to send peace on the earth. I didn't come to send peace, but a sword. For I came to set a man at odds against his father, and a daughter against her mother, and a daughter-in-law against her mother-in-law. A man's foes will be those of his own household.'" (Mt 10:34-36)

Death and resurrection of Christ

What is the history of peace and war in the Universe?

With Christ being understood as the peace for the entire Universe, the death of Christ can be understood as the loss of peace and His resurrection as restoring peace once again.

According to Hebrews 7:37 Christ "died once for all." This means that everyone has lost their peace (with God) until the return of Christ.

In other words, war has broken out throughout the entire Universe but afterward eternal peace comes.

"Christ, being raised from the dead, dies no more. Death no more has dominion over him!" (Rom. 6:9) That means that war will never return.

Christ is God conditionally

The question "Is Christ God" is similar to asking if the sequence of digits such as 2, 3, 2, 3, 2, 3… is a real number. A real number can be expressed by such a sequence and then we could say that it is a real number, but only conditionally, depending on what we mean by real numbers. (Real numbers can be defined not only as sequences of digits but also in several other ways. For example, splitting a set of rational numbers into two parts. All these ways are equivalent but different.) In like manner, Christ is conditionally God; that is, whether He is or He isn't God depends on what we mean by God.

I will sometimes use the analogy of Christ with a civilization, and sometimes the analogy of God with a civilization, depending on the context.

The Trinity is (obviously) also conditionally God. When it comes to the Trinity it is particularly clear that it is God only in a conditional sense, because clearly in general God is not a set consisting of three elements.

The scriptures plainly proclaim Christ to be God in multiple verses.

"**… Christ as concerning the flesh, who is over all, God, blessed forever. Amen.**" (Rom. 9:5)

"**… one Lord, Jesus Christ, through whom are all things, and we live through him.**" (1Cor. 8:6)

"Who is the image of the invisible God, the firstborn of all creation. For by him were all things created, in the heavens and on the earth, things visible and things invisible… He is before all things, and in him all things are held together." (Col. 1:15-17)

"For in him all the fullness of the Godhead dwells bodily." (Col. 2:9)

"… his Son… through whom also he made the worlds" (Heb. 1:2)

"His Son is the radiance of his glory, the very image of his substance, and upholding all things by the word of his power…" (Heb. 1:3)

"And, 'You, Lord, in the beginning, laid the foundation of the earth. The heavens are the works of your hands. They will perish, but you continue. They all will grow old like a garment does. As a mantle you will roll them up, And they will be changed; But you are the same. Your years will not fail.'" (Heb. 1:10-12) "Jesus Christ is the same yesterday, today, and forever." (Heb. 13:8)

"**Who, existing in the form of God, didn't consider it robbery to be equal with God.**" (Phil. 2:6)

Wouldn't taking all power and becoming "like" God be robbing God of some His power? No, it isn't.

Holy Spirit, the technology

If God is a civilization then the Holy Spirit is its technology.

Suppose someone wanted to do something with an object inside of a closed vessel. We would have trouble doing this, but a higher civilization would have the ability to move individual atoms inside of it. A force of their technology would come inside and move the individual atoms. By doing so, the subject would behave like a gas.

The technology of God is called the *Holy Spirit* (the word "spirit" may mean a gas). This is the force which is able to enter the human body and move individual atoms to, among other things, cure disease.

It is believed by many Christians that every part of God's will is accomplished by a move of the Holy Spirit. Thus, the Holy Spirit is fully (conditionally) God.

Together with above description of Christ being conditionally God this forms the Holy Trinity consisting of the Father, Son, and Holy Spirit.

The function of the Holy Spirit is *salvation;* that is repairing things, especially those things which are inside closed vessels that cannot be opened. This is because all things are done by God and the only things left in need of repair are broken things. Things that are not inside of closed vessels can be repaired by outside entities without the direct help of God.

The divinity of the Holy Spirit is a natural outcome in the civilizational consideration. Just as in our modern civilization the technology of the advanced civilization contains the totality of its knowledge.

The Holy Spirit is an active and live force: He *knows*: "**… Even so, no one knows the things of God, except God's Spirit.**" (1Cor. 2:11)

Trinity

In this civilizational approach to describing God, the doctrine of Trinity does not look contradictory or paradoxical at all.

I define a *person* as something which speaks and hears. Different persons differ in what they say and hear.

For a civilization, we would not find it contradictory to have three distinct representative agencies. (An agency is a form of a person.) Yet all three would necessarily work in agreement with each other to properly represent the civilization. This is similar to how God having three persons is not a contradiction. Three persons of God act in complete agreement, so that God is not divided.

Note that because the Father, Son, and Holy Spirit are different "agencies," we may pray to each of them. We may also pray to God without specifying a particular person. However, Jesus said we are to pray to the Father.

Don't be tricked into thinking that I am suggesting the members of the Trinity differ only in what they speak and hear. There are other differences as well. For example, the Father is greater than the Son: "**… the Father is greater than I**" (Jn. 14:28).

A prayer may be addressed to any of the three agencies officially representing God. When somebody is praying and God hears it, it differs from simply God knowing (as He knows everything), in that God's hearing of the prayer is His official reception of the information.

Sons of God

When a son grows older he becomes similar to his father. This is a definition of the word *son*.

Christ is the Son of God. This means that Christ goes to the Father. That is, He becomes the same as His Father.

Well, indeed Christ does not move. He is like a river that moves and does not move at the same time. In the same way Christ goes to His Father, but Christ does not move. The following Bible fragment says that Christ does not change:

"And, 'You, Lord, in the beginning, laid the foundation of the earth. The heavens are the works of your hands. They will perish, but you continue. They all will grow old like a garment does. As a mantle you will roll them up, And they will be changed; But you are the same. Your years will not fail.'" (Heb. 1:10-12) We are children of God, this means that our natural course of development is to become like God (Jn. 1:12).

"But as many as received him, to them he gave the right to become God's children, to those who believe in him." (Jn. 1:12)

"Behold, how great a love the Father has bestowed on us, that we should be called children of God! For this cause the world doesn't know us, because it didn't know him. Beloved, now we are

children of God, and it is not yet revealed what we will be. But we know that, when he is revealed, we will be like him; for we will see him just as he is." (1Jn. 3:1-2)

Son of man

Christ also is called *the son of man* in Gospel. This means that Christ is the final product of the development of mankind.

This is very good news because it means that the development of mankind will never be stalled but will continue without limit.

Jesus is the final result of the development of mankind. In other words, Jesus is just a guest from the infinitely far future.

It is not mankind that caused Christ to exist, instead the infinite development of mankind was made possible only by the coming of Christ to earth 2,000 years ago.

Now consider Revelation 10:6 (modified translation) **"… there will be no longer time."**

I think in this Bible verse the word *time* should be understood as an ordering of events in which preceding events can be the cause of following events but not vice versa. "No time" would mean that there is no longer an order to things, thus allowing subsequent events to affect those that come before it. In other words, unrestricted time travel is possible. I think there will be time in the sense that clocks and other physical objects dealing with time will continue to function. I think in this way, because physical objects continue to exist after Rev. 10:6 they would be unlikely to continue existing without time. Revelation 11:1 describes a temple with physical characteristics such as size; Rev. 11:13 describes an earthquake, etc. and even in Rev. 22, the last chapter of Apocalypse describes a river of water which cannot be without time as the river must flow.

A common scenario in science-fiction is members of a civilization returning back in time and changing its own development. I believe it is what Christ does with mankind.

For a loop in time this would be necessary to avoid contradictions such as the well-known paradox of somebody killing his own father before his birth by traveling in the past. I think God's commandments are intended to avoid such contradictions. For example, following the commandment "Don't kill" would make it impossible for a person to kill their father as in the mentioned paradox.

So after the second coming of Christ, we will take advantage of being part of this civilization of the highest possible development level without waiting an infinite amount of time for this. This is what "come of Christ" means.

It is worth mentioning that Islam has a very pessimistic attitude that "Allah is one and has no sons." This would mean that no one is able to reach an infinite level of development and every development will become stalled at some stage. This agrees with the Muslim belief of a "materialistic" paradise filled with the pleasures of good foods and women, rather than the infinite development towards God offered by Bible.

Christ is our hope

"**… Christ Jesus our hope.**" (1Tim. 1:1)

I would instead translate this verse "**… Christ Jesus our dream.**"

What is a dream? It is the best we can imagine. So Christ Jesus is the best we can imagine.

This is twofold:

1. Christ is good and nothing we are able to imaging can be better than Him.

2. Our common imagination is good enough to attain Christ.

Also: "**… we were saved in hope …**" (Rom. 8:24) or "**… we were saved in dream…**" It means that our salvation consists of dreams, like a table consists of wood. It also means that our dream (the best we can hope for) is exactly what we will become when our salvation is fully accomplished. We will be exactly what we hope to be. What we dream here on Earth is laid up for us in the heavens: "**because of the hope**

which is laid up for you in the heavens…" (Colossians 1:5)

Christ as the life

It is natural to think future development will only continue in the highest civilization, and that all other development outside of it will eventually stall at some point.

In other words, the highest civilization is exactly the (eternal) development.

In the Gospel development is called life. So Christ is the eternal life: "**… This is the true God, and eternal life.**" (1Jn. 5:20)

"**Jesus said to her, 'I am the resurrection and the life…'**" (Jn. 11:25)

"**Jesus said to him, 'I am the way, the truth, and the life…'**" (Jn. 14:6)

Every life is a part of Christ. Note that true life is always eternal because it is an inherent characteristic of life to continue.

All life is in Christ: "**… no longer I that live, but Christ living in me…**" (Gal. 2:20). This means that our characterization of being alive means that we are in Christ and Christ is our life.

"**He who has the Son has the life. He who doesn't have God's Son doesn't have the life.**" (1Jn. 5:12)

God

Father is greater than Christ: "**… the Father is greater than I.**" (Jn. 14:28)

It can be understood this way: Christ is peace (see above), but "**… God is love …**" (1Jn. 4:8, 16). Love is more than just peace, because peace is nothing more than the absence of war but love is something greater. If we have love with somebody we also necessarily have peace with him, but the reverse is not always true. Consider the case of North and South Korea today. They have had peace since the armistice of 1953, yet one would be a fool to say that both sides love each other.

As God is love, all of the following applies to God:

"Love is patient and is kind; love doesn't envy. Love doesn't brag, is not proud, doesn't behave itself inappropriately, doesn't seek its own way, is not provoked, takes no account of evil; doesn't rejoice in unrighteousness, but rejoices with the truth; bears all things, believes all things, hopes all things, endures all things. Love never fails..." (1Cor. 13:4-8)

Note that while God being love results in kindness to those who are in Him, He is cruel towards outsiders (those who are not in the Peace), as they are His military opponents.

"See then the goodness and severity of God. Toward those who fell, severity; but toward you, goodness, if you continue in his goodness; otherwise you also will be cut off." (Rom. 11:22)

Despite their being one God, the desires of Christ are different than the desires of the Father:

"**He went forward a little, fell on his face, and prayed, saying, 'My Father, if it is possible, let this cup pass away from me; nevertheless, not what I desire, but what you desire.'**" (Mt. 26:39)

"**He said, 'Abba, Father, all things are possible to you. Please remove this cup from me. However, not what I desire, but what you desire.'**" (Mrk. 14:36) "**Saying, 'Father, if you are willing, remove this cup from me. Nevertheless, not my will, but yours, be done.'**" (Luk. 22:42)

"**… called God his own Father, making himself equal with God.**" (Jn. 5:18) In my opinion, "making himself equal with God" means the following formula:

$$f(f) = God, \text{ where f is Christ.}$$

Unity of the Trinity

Christ and Father are one entity:

"**I and the Father are one.**" (Jn. 10:30)

"**Jesus therefore answered them, 'Most assuredly, I tell you, the Son can do nothing of

himself, but what he sees the Father doing. For whatever things he does, these the Son also does likewise.'" (Jn. 5:19)

In other words, the Son cannot do anything independently of the Father. They are not independent entities but they do everything in union and complete harmony with each other, so that they are one entity rather than two distinct ones.

"I can of myself do nothing…" (Jn. 5:30)

"… I do nothing of myself, but as my Father taught me…" (Jn. 8:28)

"… that they may be one, even as we are." (Jn. 17:11)

God is a time machine

So, we conclude that there will one day be a "time lift" a time machine able to travel in time but not below a given start time (the time of the Second Advent). Traveling from the future to the time before the Second Advent is possible but very hard.

"And tasted the good word of God, and the powers of the age to come." (Heb. 6:5)

Notice that there are some similarities between God and time machines.

Contradictions with time machines

Suppose we have a time machine. We will consider the following case and take it to a logical contradiction:

At 10:00PM we get and read a piece of paper which we receive from the time machine. If the number is 0, then after an hour (at 11:00PM) we put a piece of paper with the number 1 to the time machine and transfer it back an hour. If the number we received at 10:00PM is 1 then we put the number 0 on a piece of paper and transfer it back an hour.

Now we have an obvious logical contradiction: If the number is 0 it is 1, if the number is 1 it is 0.

So for a time machine to work (not be contradictory), we must not put it to such a test.

It is similar to the biblical commandment not to test God. This I the reason I feel that God and time machines are similar, or perhaps even related.

If we were to attempt to test a time machine in this way either the machine will not work, or we would be removed from presence of the time machine by some force. Compare this with the following verses.

"… it is written, 'You shall not test the Lord, your God.'" (Mt. 4:7)

"It has been said, 'You shall not tempt the Lord your God.'" (Luk. 4:12)

"Neither let us test the Lord, as some of them tested, and perished by the serpents." (1Cor. 10:9)

Here is another example of a contradiction incompatible with the presence of a time machine. If you travel into the past and killed your own father before your conception, this would also lead to a contradiction. You were born (otherwise you cannot go into the time machine), but then if you kill your father you are not born. If you are not born then how can you go back in time and kill your father? Compare it with this verse:

"as knowing this, that law is not made for a righteous man, but for the lawless and insubordinate, for the ungodly and sinners, for the unholy and profane, for murderers of fathers and murderers of mothers…" (1Tim. 1:9)

Time machine as a hard problem solver

A time machine can solve what is called NP-hard problems by mathematicians. Don't worry if you don't understand this term. I will explain it by use of a simple example, a chess game. (Don't worry, if you don't understand this example due to not knowing the rules, just believe my conclusion that if you are inside a time machine it can mysteriously make your brain unbeatable in chess competitions, just like you received revelations about every move. This is, of course, not only about chess but the idea that being inside of a time machine would enable you to receive revelations about all manner of difficult problems.)

The following is the way to win in chess using a time machine:

1. Receive a piece of paper with a record of a chess party from the time machine (see the future).

2. Start to play chess.

3. If you won (in the future) repeat the same moves you received in the piece of paper.

4. If you lost, make some other moves.

5. Using the machine return a piece of paper with the moves you made into the past.

Voila! The laws of logic lead to a scenario where you won (otherwise the future moves you received would be different than the moves you make while inside the time machine, but this is impossible because you are making the moves you received which are the same as moves you are doing).

Isn't this similar to receiving a revelation from God?

Another similarity between a time machine and God: God offers unlimited possibilities, and a time machine would likewise also present unlimited possibilities regarding technologies of the future. God can predict the future and so can the time machine.

Other

Conclusion: God is a time machine.

"Jesus therefore said to them again, 'Most assuredly, I tell you, I am the sheep's door'" (Jn. 10:7)

"I am the door…" (Jn. 10:9)

What is the purpose of a door? It separates two particular spaces from each other. It also enables a person to travel from one of these spaces to another. If this is the case, then doesn't this mean that Christ is a hyperspace portal?

"But now in Christ Jesus you who once were far off are made near in the blood of Christ." (Eph. 2:13)

Might this mean that Christ is the conduit that provides a shortcut through the universe? In Einstein's Theory of General Relativity that would be a hyperspace portal.

Chapter 5 Jesus' life on Earth

Jesus Christ is an avatar of God. This means that the acts of Jesus Christ were the most efficient possible. If He played chess, he would win over any other adversary. (However He most probably never played chess.)

"I indeed baptize you in water for repentance, but he who comes after me is mightier than I, whose shoes I am not worthy to carry. He will baptize you in the Holy Spirit." (Mt. 3:11)

"He preached, saying, "After me comes he who is mightier than I, the thong of whose sandals I am not worthy to stoop down and loosen." (Mrk. 1:7)

"John answered them all, "I indeed baptize you with water, but he comes who is mightier than I, the latchet of whose sandals I am not worthy to loosen…" (Luke 3:16)

"He is the one who comes after me, who is preferred before me, whose sandal strap I'm not worthy to loosen." (Jn. 1:27)

This means that John the Baptizer was not even able to carry out the task of carrying shoes efficiently enough to be worthy to do so in the presence of Jesus. This is in spite of Jesus saying that John was the greatest of men (at least of these who were before Jesus).

"Most assuredly I tell you, among those who are born of women there has not arisen anyone greater than John the Baptizer; yet he who is least in the Kingdom of Heaven is greater than he." (Mt. 11:11)

"For I tell you, among those who are born of women there is not a greater prophet than John the Baptizer, yet he who is least in the Kingdom of God is greater than he." (Luk. 7:28)

(Who does Jesus mean by the least in the Kingdom of Heaven? It could refer to the least of the angels, but perhaps it refers to the least of those saved after Christ's death.)

"**Then Jesus came from Galilee to the Jordan to John, to be baptized by him. But John would have hindered him, saying, 'I need to be baptized by you, and you come to me?' But Jesus, answering, said to him, 'Allow it now, for this is the fitting way for us to fulfill all righteousness.' Then he allowed him.**" (Mt. 3:13-15)

It is just my guess, but I suspect that it was a "reverse baptism." The water of the world was baptized by Jesus, rather than Jesus being baptized by water, for the purpose of making water to better be able to baptize us.

"**At that time, Jesus went on the Sabbath day through the grain fields. His disciples were hungry and began to pluck heads of grain and to eat. But the Pharisees, when they saw it, said to him, 'Behold, your disciples do what is not lawful to do on the Sabbath.'**" (Mt. 12:1-2)

"It happened that he was going on the Sabbath day through the grain fields, and his disciples began, as they went, to pluck the ears of grain. The Pharisees said to him, 'Behold, why do they do that which is not lawful on the Sabbath day?'" (Mrk 2:23-24; Luk. 6:1-2)

Note that He allowed His disciples to do it, but He strictly followed the law, refusing to violate it even in the slightest.

How did Jesus perform His wonders? He laid aside his divine power and did the wonders only through the power of the Holy Spirit. He did so to be our example; the common man would not be able to use divine power to do mighty works on their own, and neither would Jesus.

"Jesus, full of the Holy Spirit…" (Luk. 4:1)

"Jesus returned in the power of the Spirit into Galilee…" (Luk. 4:14)

This means that by the Holy Spirit, Jesus has access to the force to raise tons with His hands. Read in my book "End of Gospel" how I (for a limited amount of time) had a similar power.

Incarnation of Jesus

In my opinion, God being incarnated in Jesus means the following: He decided to make a man who does the most efficient acts possible, but with reasoning limited to these facts which the man (Jesus) is able to see or hear with human senses. God decided to limit Christ's acts into this man form for the human life of Jesus.

Jesus possessed not only the five human senses but also telepathy.

"Immediately Jesus, perceiving in his spirit that they so reasoned within themselves, said to them, 'Why do you reason these things in your hearts?'" (Mrk 2:8)

"Jesus, knowing their thoughts, said, 'Why do you think evil in your hearts?'" (Mt. 9:4)

"Knowing their thoughts, Jesus said to them…" (Mt. 12:25)

"Jesus, perceiving the reasoning of their hearts…" (Luk. 9:47)

"He brought him to Jesus. Jesus looked at him, and said, 'You are Simon the son of Jonah. You shall be called Cephas' (which is by interpretation, Peter)." (Jn. 1:42)

See also Jn. 1:47-50; 4:17-18; 6:61. He (using telepathy), knew all men living on the Earth.

"But Jesus didn't trust himself to them, because he knew everyone, and because he didn't need for anyone to testify concerning man; for he himself knew what was in man." (Jn. 2:24-25)

If Jesus wasn't limited to information from human senses, He wouldn't have needed to *hear* that John was delivered up in order to know that it occurred.

"Now when Jesus heard that John was delivered up, he withdrew into Galilee." (Mt. 4:12)

However, there is a different explanation for why He needed to hear it (if He knew all). He may have wanted for others to hear it before going to Galilee.

He heard it at the same time as the others, so this meant that He was doing it only after others heard this news. However this explanation seems unlikely for me, and I instead suppose that Jesus' decisions were limited by information received from human senses. Christ knows everything, but He made a conscious choice not to use all of this information he had access to, choosing instead to rely solely on the human senses in control of Jesus.

"The Jews therefore marveled, saying, 'How does this man know letters, having never been educated?'" (Jn. 7:15)

He knew everything that happened before His birth. **"Now, Father, glorify me with your own self with the glory which I had with you before the world existed."** (Jn. 17:5)

One thing He did with His unlimited mind was to calculate the number of hairs on the heads of His disciples.

"But the very hairs of your head are all numbered." (Mt. 10:30)

"**But the very hairs of your head are all numbered…**" (Luk. 12:7)

Jesus remembered His life before the incarnation. "**Yet I tell you that even Solomon in all his glory was not dressed like one of these**" (Mt. 6:29)

"**Consider the lilies, how they grow. They don't toil, neither do they spin; yet I tell you, even Solomon in all his glory was not arrayed like one of these.**" (Luk. 12:27)

Notice in these verses He says he remembers meeting King Solomon.

Why did Jesus has allowed the demons to go to into a herd of pigs? Mrk. 5:12-13; Luk. 8:32-33 A possible explanation is to make it known to us that demons are real and that they may enter pigs.

"**He didn't allow him, but said to him, 'Go to your house, to your friends, and tell them what great things the Lord has done for you, and how he had mercy on you.'**" (Mrk. 5:19)

Sometimes Jesus asked questions:

"**He asked the scribes, 'What are you asking them?'**" (Mrk. 9:16)

"**He said to them, 'What do you want me to do for you?'**" (Mrk. 10:36)

This doesn't mean that Jesus didn't know the answer. He just wanted to make the person He questioned speak up so others could hear the answer.

"**They rose up, threw him out of the city, and led him to the brow of the hill that their city was built on, that they might throw him off the cliff. But he, passing through the midst of them, went his way.**" (Luk. 4:29-30)

"**Therefore they took up stones to throw at him, but Jesus was hidden, and went out of the temple, having gone through the midst of them, and so passed by**." (Jn. 8:59)

I think this means that Jesus moved with such great skill through the crowd that they were led by him to disturb each other in an attempt to catch Him.

"No one has ascended into heaven, but he who descended out of heaven, the Son of Man, who is in heaven." (Jn. 3:13)

This means that Christ remained in heaven even when He was visiting the Earth. (Could it be otherwise with the electromagnetic waves of the Universe?)

"But Jesus answered them, 'My Father is still working, so I am working, too.'" (Jn. 5:17)

So the theological theory that God presented Himself only as the Father, then only as the Son, and then only as Holy Spirit is wrong. Both the Father and Son worked at the same time.

Temptation of Jesus

"Then Jesus was led up by the Spirit into the wilderness to be tempted by the devil." (Mt. 4:1)

"He was there in the wilderness forty days tempted by Satan…" (Mrk. 1:13)

"… being tempted by the devil…" (Luk. 4:2)

"**For we don't have a high priest who can't be touched with the feeling of our infirmities, but one who has been in all points tempted like we are, yet without sin.**" (Heb. 4:15)

"**For in that he himself has suffered being tempted, he is able to help those who are tempted.**" (Heb. 2:18)

Why was Jesus tempted? He always makes the right decisions and thus never could fall into a temptation. The answer is He was tempted so that others (people, angels, and so on) could see and learn from His responses to temptation.

This world and the evil in it exist with a purpose: Various situations present themselves for us should we be tempted. If we pass through a temptation, it is to set the world free from a particular wrong mode of action committed by certain kinds of persons. We need to overcome temptations with faith. Using our faith to set us free from a temptation is essential.

Why Jesus refused to kneel before Devil

"Again, the devil took him to an exceedingly high mountain, and showed him all the kingdoms of the world, and their glory. He said to him, 'I will give you all of these things, if you will fall down and worship me.'" (Mt. 4:8-9)

Jesus refused to accept this offer of the Devil.

Have you ever wondered why Jesus refused this offer by the Devil? Think about what he was asking. Satan was willing to give all of his earthly power to Jesus if he would only bow the knee one time. He didn't even place any conditions on how long Jesus had to bow. Jesus could have bowed for less than a second and the devil would have given him the world. So why didn't he take what would seem to be an incredible bargain? After all, couldn't he have done so more as a formality like bowing in the presence of royalty without actually engaging in worship? All that would change would be the position of his body, not his heart.

I'd compare the interactions of Jesus Christ and the Devil to rivals in a chess game. One of the key elements of a chess game is the concept of sacrificing a valuable piece to obtain victory. It is in this light that the reason for Christ's refusal can be inferred by the next move. "**Then Jesus said to him, Satan, go behind me…**" (Mt. 4:10)

"**Jesus answered him, 'Get behind me Satan! For it is written, 'You shall worship the Lord your God, and him only shall you serve.'**" (Luk. 4:8)

By this bold statement Jesus reveals that he was the leader and all Satan can do is lead from behind. He said that the Devil will follow after him. What Jesus did here was take the time and attention of the Devil which he could have used to tempt others instead of wasting his time on Jesus who cannot be tempted.

If Jesus were to have agreed to do what the Devil required, the Devil would then have been able to count his operation with Jesus as being complete and then go on to tempt other people instead of his focusing his attention on useless attempts to tempt Jesus.

Moreover, as these verses make clear, by Satan obeying Jesus (unwillingly) he was actually serving ("worshiped" as said in this Bible verse) Christ (as Christ is God). In other words by going after Jesus, Satan ended up having to do what Jesus required of him, despite his best attempts to do otherwise.

An important thing to note here is that although the Devil tried to *tempt* Jesus, He didn't *tempt* the Devil by causing him to have the wrong opinion on anything. All Jesus did was to spend time with the Devil. If your friend (or enemy) came to your house and did something to cause him to remain in your house as long as possible, this could not rightfully be called a temptation.

Jesus was in the Hell

After His death, Jesus was in Hell. Hell is literally under the Earth. (I suppose that Hell is the movement of Earth's magnetic core.)

"For as Jonah was three days and three nights in the belly of the whale, so will the Son of Man be three days and three nights in the heart of the earth." (Mt. 12:40)

"In which he also went and preached to the spirits in prison." (1Pet. 3:19)

"For to this end was the gospel preached even to the dead, that they might be judged indeed as men in the flesh, but live as to God in the spirit." (1Pet. 4:6)

"Jesus said to him, 'Assuredly I tell you, today you will be with me in Paradise.'" (Luk. 23:43 Jesus is talking to a condemned criminal on the cross next to him who repented.)

What these passages mean is that contrary to the belief of Russian Orthodoxes there is no elapsed time between death and when a soul enters paradise. Also note that Jesus was in both paradise and Hell at the same time: **"He who descended is the one who also ascended far above all the heavens, that he might fill all things. Now this, He ascended, what is it but** that he also first descended into the lower parts of the earth? He who descended is the one who also ascended far above all the heavens, that he might fill all things." (Eph. 4:9, 10)

Chapter 6   Salvation

What is sin?
Sin in Old Testament

(Here the modified translation from [Without Vowels wiki](#) are used.)

Before Adam's and Eve's fall into sin, people were able to perform calculations with their brains just like powerful computers. It is clear from the following verses that things on earth were once vastly different:

"**God saw everything that he had made, and, behold, it was very good…**" (Gen. 1:31)

"**And was perfect the heaven and the Earth and all their army.**" (Gen. 2:1, modified translation) or even "**And was perfect the heaven and the Earth and their army was calculating.**"

"**And both Adam and his wife were talented and were not ashamed each other.**" (Gen. 2:25, modified translation)

"Out of the ground Yahweh God made every tree to grow that is pleasant to the sight, and good for food; the tree of life also in the midst of the garden, and the tree of the knowledge of good and evil." (Gen. 2:9)

In the garden of Eden there were trees of knowledge. You could eat a fruit and instantly learn quantum mechanics.

One of the trees was the tree of knowledge of good and bad. This fruit injected knowledge into the human brain of how the brain itself functions (what it says is good and what is bad). This knowledge caused the brain to trick itself, effectively causing a short-circuit. This is somehow similar to giving a program the password to a computer, thus allowing inviting it in to destroy the normal functionality of the computer (as well as to destroy itself). More specifically, the brain starts seeking to do what makes it feel better rather than engaging in its proper purpose.

"But of the tree of the knowledge of good and evil, you shall not eat of it: for in the day that you eat of it you will surely die." (Gen. 2:17)

Certainly, to die here is not referring to a physical death, instead it is talking about crashing the person's "operating system."

"… she took of the fruit of it, and ate; and she gave some to her husband with her, and he ate. Both of their eyes were opened, and they knew that they were naked…" (Gen. 3:6-7) Before the fall, when Adam and Eve were together only one of them needed to keep their eyes opened because there was a wireless link between their brains and each was seeing through the eyes of the partner. After the fall, the wireless network crashed and they both needed to open their eyes.

"God said: We will create man in our image as our likeness. He will descent to the level of fishes of the Ocean, and birds of the sky, and beasts of the entire Earth, and all reptiles creeping on the Earth." (Gen. 1:26, modified translation)

This means that people would lose their computing power.

Sin in the New Testament

"**But sin, finding occasion through the commandment, produced in me all kinds of coveting. For apart from the law, sin is dead. I was alive apart from the law once, but when the commandment came, sin revived, and I died. The commandment, which was for life, this I found to be for death; for sin, finding occasion through the commandment, deceived me, and through it killed me. Therefore the law indeed is holy, and the commandment holy, and righteous, and good. Did then that which is good become death to me? May it never be! But sin, that it might be shown to be sin, by working death to me through that which is good; that through the commandment sin might become exceeding sinful.**" (Rom 7:8-11)

"**Did then that which is good become death to me? May it never be! But sin, that it might be shown to be sin, by working death to me through**

that which is good; that through the commandment sin might become exceeding sinful." (Rom. 7:13)

This means that sin is a desire to do the opposite of what is good. It makes evil that which is good.

Sin is the following:

"**I find then the law, that, to me, while I desire to do good, evil is present.**" (Rom. 7:21)

"**For he who has died has been freed from sin.**" (Rom. 6:7)

Our brain does not have enough computing power to overcome sin (which is a *denial of service attack* as a computer hacker would say). But when we die, our personality is transferred to a much more powerful computer run by God, so that the sin in us is overcome.

"**For to me to live is Christ, and to die is gain.**" (Phil. 1:21)

"But I am in a dilemma between the two, having the desire to depart and be with Christ, which is far better." (Phil. 1:23)

As every of us has his own individual defects, God will write for every of us a new operating system specifically tailored for a particular person to overcome our defects:

"Therefore if anyone is in Christ, he is a new creation. The old things have passed away. Behold, all things have become new." (2Cor. 5:17)

Every one of us is a new creation.

God made Christ to be sin, in order that He would enter into us and live in our sinful bodies:

"For him who knew no sin he made to be sin on our behalf…" (2Cor. 5:21)

The processes ("works") in the brain of a sinner die and uselessly occupy memory, so there remains no memory for current works of the brain:

"… not laying again a foundation of repentance from dead works, of faith toward God." (Heb. 6:1)

"**… will the blood of Christ… cleanse your conscience from dead works to serve the living God?**" (Hebrews 9:14)

This problem is solved by faith.

"**Because you say, 'I am rich, and have gotten riches, and have need of nothing;' and don't know that you are the wretched one, miserable, poor, blind, and naked.**" (Rev. 3:17)

Tongue

Our brain's speech center is a source of evil. It pushes evil ways of thinking into the entire brain.

"**And the tongue is a fire. The world of iniquity among our members is the tongue, which defiles the whole body, and sets on fire the course of nature, and is set on fire by Gehenna.**" (Jam. 3:6)

"**Do all things without murmurings…**" (Phil. 2:14)

Murmuring is an action of tongue. Flee from it.

"For in many things we all stumble. If anyone doesn't stumble in word, the same is a perfect man, able to bridle the whole body also." (Jam. 3:2)

"But nobody can tame the tongue. It is a restless evil, full of deadly poison." (Jam. 3:8)

So learn to think without pronouncing your thoughts inside of yourselves. This brings a great wisdom. As a mathematician I can confirm this.

You can read more about sin and salvation in my book "End of Gospel", especially the chapter "Real Superman" which talks about how for an entire month I was completely freed from sin and transformed into a computer.

Faith and deeds

"That whoever believes in him [Christ] should not perish, but have eternal life." (Jn. 3:15, 16)

"One who believes in the Son has eternal life…" (Jn 3:36)

"Most assuredly, I tell you, he who believes in me has eternal life." (Jn 6:47) Note that this refers to *every* believer not just some special "saints" or those people who do many good deeds.

It is a false teaching that after death everybody comes to God's court.

"He who believes in him is not judged. He who doesn't believe has been judged already, because he has not believed in the name of the one and only Son of God." (Jn. 3:18)

"Most assuredly I tell you, he who hears my word, and believes him who sent me, has eternal life, and doesn't come into judgment, but has passed out of death into life." (Jn. 5:24)

Salvation is not by personal works, but nevertheless salvation is by deeds; the deeds of God.

"Jesus answered them, 'This is the work of God, that you believe in him whom he has sent.'" (Jn. 6:29) That which for people is faith, is a deed for God.

"We maintain therefore that a man is justified by faith apart from the works of the law." (Rom. 3:28)

Martin Luther brought about the Reformation by bringing to the masses who did not have ready access to the Bible that they are justified by their faith, not by works. As Luther said, even if you were to commit 100 adulteries and 100 killings in a day, this cannot separate you from grace. If a person's works were an integral part of their salvation then there would be no reason for Christ's death.

"For if those who are of the law are heirs, faith is made void, and the promise is made of no effect." (Rom. 4:14)

"And if by grace, then it is no longer of works; otherwise grace is no longer grace. But if it is of works, it is no longer grace; otherwise work is no longer work." (Rom. 11:6)

"Yet knowing that a man is not justified by the works of the law but through the faith of Jesus Christ, even we believed in Christ Jesus, that we

might be justified by faith in Christ, and not by the works of the law, because no flesh will be justified by the works of the law." (Gal. 2:16)

"**Wiping out the handwriting in ordinances which was against us; and he has taken it out of the way, nailing it to the cross.**" (Col. 2:14)

"**For by grace you have been saved through faith, and that not of yourselves; it is the gift of God, not of works, that no one would boast.**" (Eph. 2:8, 9)

Again, our works cannot bring about our salvation. If this is the case some may ask, does this mean that good deeds are not important? No, the Bible goes on to say that is the reason God saved us.

"**For we are his workmanship, created in Christ Jesus for good works, which God prepared before that we would walk in them.**" (Eph. 2:10)

The *purpose* of our salvation is to do good deeds.

Faith without deeds is dead:

"What good is it, my brothers, if a man says he has faith, but has no works? Can faith save him?" (Jam. 2:14)

"Even so faith, if it has no works, is dead in itself." (Jam. 2:17)

See also James 2:20-26. Taken together these verses reveal that faith is demonstrated by works. If there are no good works, there is no true faith.

What is the Gospel?

The word "Gospel" literally means "good news" or rather "correct news." It also can be translated as "good or correct behavior of angels."

This means, that Gospel is the written good order (for angels) to distribute news; so Christ comes first and sin last, thus focusing our attention on good news, rather than bad news. It is just like blocking out news for terrorists in order for terror not to materialize.

During the 1970s in America there was an epidemic of terrorist attacks and hijackings. After each event a group would call in and take credit for it. The news media would diligently report the news by proclaiming the group who took credit for the bombing. Then the media realized that by doing this they were encouraging these groups and others to do similar acts in order to get the publicity. They then collectively decided to no longer print or broadcast the names of the groups or persons who did the attack. Within a very short time the bombings stopped.

In the world above where angels live the news comes first and events are second. Events depend on news rather than the news relying on events. Thus we need good news.

The mission of the saints

"Then Jesus said to him, 'Put your sword back into its place, for all those who take the sword will die by the sword.'" (Mt. 26:52)

"… If anyone is with the sword, he must be killed. Here is the endurance and the faith of the saints." (Rev. 13:10)

Saints were created by God, who gave them faith with a specific mission to keep peace in the heavens. Saints are created to keep one particular principle: "If anyone is with the sword, he must be killed" that is to stop any war. This may seem like a simple principle, but putting it into practice can be extremely difficult and involves many different areas of service. The word "endurance" in Rev. 13:10 signifies that one needs endurance to be able to engage in many different facets of war and keep peace in all situations.

This also pertains to those who use the word of God as a sword. We should pray peacefully:

"Bless those who persecute you; bless, and don't curse." (Rom. 12:14)

"But the Jerusalem that is above is free, which is the mother of us all." (Gal. 4:26)

This verse refers to a city in heaven. The word Jerusalem translates as "a city of peace." Jerusalem is a capital city in heaven, and its purpose is to keep peace in heaven. It is our mother because we were created after its task (to keep peace).

"But now they desire a better country, that is, a heavenly one. Therefore God is not ashamed of them, to be called their God, for he has prepared a city for them." (Heb. 11:16)

"But you have come to Mount Zion, and to the city of the living God, the heavenly Jerusalem, and to innumerable hosts of angels." (Heb. 12:22)

The earthly Jerusalem was also created with the same purpose, to keep peace. But as we can see, it has not yet fulfilled this purpose.

"Blessed are the peacemakers, For they shall be called children of God." (Mt. 5:9)

This means that "children of God" are the same as "peacemakers" (in heaven).

"Now may the Lord of peace himself give you peace at all times in all ways. The Lord be with you all." (2Thes. 3:16)

Christ as our righteousness

Christ was made our righteousness:

"But of him, you are in Christ Jesus, who was made to us... righteousness..." (1Cor. 1:30)

What does this mean? It means that to be our righteousness, one needs to be as great as Christ (to present us as righteous despite our sins is so difficult that the power of Christ is required to do it). But this also means that Christ's sacrifice is enough for God to consider us as righteous.

Christ is in us:

"To whom God was pleased to make known what are the riches of the glory of this mystery among the Gentiles, which is Christ in you, the hope of glory" (Col. 1:27)

"... Or don't you know as to your own selves, that Jesus Christ is in you?—unless indeed you are disqualified." (2Cor. 13:5)

If Christ is in us, then His righteousness is in us, and this overweighs our sins. So if Christ is in us, we are righteous.

The judgment of God is not unjust. He judges us according to our *real* righteousness which is Christ in us, not just a "declared" righteousness.

So the Eastern Orthodox doctrine of salvation by having more than 50 percent good deeds is indeed true, as long as Christ is in us then his infinite righteousness overweighs our sins and we are one hundred percent righteous. If Christ is not in us, then we are not righteous at all but are complete sinners.

Predestination vs free will

The following verses confirm predestination in salvation:

"All those who the Father gives me will come to me. Him who comes to me I will in no way throw out." (Jn. 6:37)

"No one can come to me unless the Father who sent me draws him, and I will raise him up in the last day." (Jn. 6:44)

"He said, 'For this cause have I said to you that no one can come to me, unless it is given to him by my Father.'" (Jn. 6:65)

"You didn't choose me, but I chose you, and appointed you, that you should go and bear fruit, and that your fruit should remain…" (Jn. 15:16)

"For whom he foreknew, he also predestined to be conformed to the image of his Son… Whom he predestined, those he also called. Whom he called, those he also justified. Whom he justified, those he also glorified." (Rom. 8:29-30)

"Having predestined us for adoption as children through Jesus Christ to himself, according to the good pleasure of his desire, to the praise of the glory of his grace, by which he freely bestowed favor on us in the Beloved." (Eph. 1:5-6)

Can predestination be reconciled with a person having free choice? I think it can, and the verse which resolves it is Isaiah 65:24. "**It shall happen that, before they call, I will answer…**" God heard our call to Him before the world was created.

Thus evangelism is just an outer appearance of salvation, which depends solely on God's call.

"**He answered them, 'I tell you that if these were silent, the stones would cry out.'**" (Luk. 19:40)

If we were to stop preaching, salvation would still continue to happen.

We should strive *not* to be saved

"**He who loves his soul will lose it. He who hates his soul in this world will keep it to eternal life.**" (Jn. 12:25, refined translation)

"**He who finds his soul will lose it; and he who loses his soul for my sake will find it.**" (Mt. 10:39, refined translation)

"For whoever desires to save his soul will lose it, and whoever will lose his soul for my sake will find it." (Mt. 16:25, refined translation)

"Whoever seeks to save his soul loses it, but whoever loses his soul preserves it." (Luke. 17:33, refined translation)

"He called the multitude to himself with his disciples, and said to them, "Whoever wants to come after me, let him deny himself, and take up his cross, and follow me. For whoever wants to save his soul will lose it; and whoever will lose his soul for my sake and the gospel's will save it." (Mrk. 8:34-35, refined translation)

"For whoever desires to save his soul will lose it, but whoever will lose his soul for my sake, the same will save it." (Luk. 9:24, refined translation)

"For everyone who exalts himself will be humbled, and whoever humbles himself will be exalted." (Luk. 14:11)

"**… for everyone who exalts himself will be humbled, but he who humbles himself will be exalted.**" (Luk. 18:14)

"**He must increase, but I must decrease.**" (Jn. 3:30)

As I've described above, our salvation is by predestination and this cannot be changed. That being said, our purpose should not be just to get to heaven but to bring to heaven as little of our human character as possible. In other words, we need to hate our souls in this world. The purpose of salvation is to cleanse us from our sinful character traits as much as possible by teaching us to deny ourselves. Not the salvation itself, but this cleansing has value.

Salvation in the Old Testament

About Herod killing all the young boys in Israel:

"**Then that which was spoken by Jeremiah the prophet was fulfilled, saying, 'A voice was heard in Ramah, Lamentation, weeping and great**

mourning, Rachel weeping for her children; She wouldn't be comforted, Because they are no more.'" (Mt. 2:17-18)

Based on this verse, it seems evident that the spirit of Rachel was alive at the time Herod killed the children. She was worried about things happening on the Earth. This means the Roman Catholic doctrine of saints in heaven participating in the life of people on the Earth is not a lie.

One more example of sins being forgiven *before* the death and resurrection of Jesus:

"Behold, they brought to him a man who was paralyzed, lying on a bed. Jesus, seeing their faith, said to the paralytic, 'Son, cheer up! Your sins are forgiven you.'" (Mt. 9:2)

"Jesus, seeing their faith, said to the paralytic, 'Son, your sins are forgiven you.'" (Mrk. 2:5; Luk. 5:20)

Abel speaks after his death:

"By faith, Abel… and through it he, being dead, still speaks." (Heb. 11:4)

"The tombs were opened, and many bodies of the saints who had fallen asleep were raised. And coming out of the tombs after his resurrection, they entered into the holy city and appeared to many." (Mt. 27:52-53)

There were saints who died *before* the death and resurrection of Jesus Christ.

Luke 16:19-25 plainly shows that Lazarus and Abraham were both in paradise *before* the death and resurrection of Jesus. And Bible does not say that it was a proverb.

"And all ate the same spiritual food; and all drank the same spiritual drink. For they drank of a spiritual rock that followed them, and the rock was Christ." (1Cor. 10:3-4)

They were partakers of Christ even though He hadn't yet come to earth in bodily form. Yet they were able to be saved by Christ just like those who lived afterward.

Stars

The spirits of saved people will be placed into stars.

"**Then the righteous will shine forth like the sun in the kingdom of their Father. He who has ears to hear, let him hear.**" (Mt. 13:43)

"**Many of those who sleep in the dust of the earth shall awake, some to everlasting life, and some to shame and everlasting contempt. Those who are wise shall shine as the brightness of the expanse; and those who turn many to righteousness as the stars forever and ever.**" (Dan. 12:2, 3)

Commandments

I teach that we should not attempt to artificially change our habits to follows the Bible's commandments. Instead, our inner nature should be changed and this should happen by itself so that we follow commandments naturally without specifically setting our mind to follow a particular commandment.

If we focus too much on fulfilling some particular commandment, it may lead us to violate other commandments. If we continue to stuff things into a filled bag, eventually something will need to come out to free up more space.

"You blind guides, who strain out a gnat, and swallow a camel!" (Mt. 23:24)

The solution is not to put too many things into a small bag, but instead make the bag bigger. Follow love and faith, not a particular commandment.

While faith is the ultimate goal, God **"remembered they were but flesh"** (Psalm 78:39). In other words, God understands that we are subject to human failings. Because of this he established his commandments not as means of salvation, but as guideposts to live by until our level of maturity is able to directly apply the principles of faith and love.

"Having abolished in the flesh the hostility, the law of commandments contained in ordinances…" (Eph. 2:15)

"One who has my commandments, and keeps them, that person is one who loves me…" (Jn. 14:21)

Keeping Christ's commandments is a criterion of our love to Him.

"This is how we know that we know him: if we keep his commandments. One who says, 'I know him,' and doesn't keep his commandments, is a liar, and the truth isn't in him." (1Jn. 2:3-4)

"By this we know that we love the children of God, when we love God and keep his commandments." (1Jn. 5:2)

"This is love, that we should walk according to his commandments…" (2Jn. 1:6)

Whether we fulfill any particular commandment without hypocrisy is whether or not our mind and heart are set right. It isn't a purpose to strive, but a criterion of the true purpose. When we become what we should be, the commandments are fulfilled "automatically."

"**Whoever, therefore, shall break one of these least commandments, and teach others to do so, shall be called least in the Kingdom of Heaven; but whoever shall do and teach them shall be called great in the Kingdom of Heaven.**" (Mt. 5:19)

Whether we fulfill the commandments or not is the criterion of how big or small we are in the Kingdom of Heaven.

"**But if you are led by the Spirit, you are not under the law.**" (Gal. 5:18)

"**But I tell you, don't resist him who is evil; but whoever strikes you on your right cheek, turn to him the other also.**" (Mt. 5:39)

"**But I tell you who hear: love your enemies, do good to those who hate you, bless those who curse you, and pray for those who mistreat you. To him who strikes you on the cheek, offer also the other; and from him who takes away your cloak, don't withhold your coat also.**" (Luk. 6:27-29)

This means that we should not resist a person who disturbs us to do good works for the world. Our purpose is not to do good for the world.

"Don't love the world, neither the things that are in the world. If anyone loves the world, the Father's love isn't in him." (1Jn. 2:15)

If somebody damages your mouth so that you cannot speak and proclaim the Gospel because of your broken mouth, rather than resist him, in humility you should accept that this time God has not given you the task to preach with your mouth.

"But I tell you, love your enemies, bless those who curse you, do good to those who hate you, and pray for those who mistreat you and persecute you, that you may be children of your Father who is in heaven. For he makes his sun to rise on the evil and the good, and sends rain on the just and the unjust." (Mt. 5:44-45)

Being the children of your Father in heaven means not doing good in this world, because otherwise not resisting your enemies (people who disturb you to do good) would be contrary to your purpose.

Do you know that Bible allows you to steal if you are hungry?

"**But he said to them, 'Haven't you read what David did, when he was hungry, and those who were with him; how he entered into the house of God, and ate the show bread, which was not lawful for him to eat, neither for those who were with him, but only for the priests?'**" (Mt. 12:3-4)

"**He said to them, 'Did you never read what David did, when he had need, and was hungry—he, and they who were with him? How he entered into the house of God when Abiathar was high priest, and ate the show bread, which it is not lawful to eat except for the priests, and gave also to those who were with him?'**" (Mrk 2:25-26)

"**Jesus, answering them, said, 'Haven't you read what David did when he was hungry, he, and those who were with him; how he entered into the house of God, and took and ate the show bread,** and gave also to those who were with him, which is not lawful to eat except for the priests alone?'"** (Luk. 6:3-4)

Temptations

"**Count it all joy, my brothers, when you fall into various temptations, knowing that the testing of your faith produces endurance. Let endurance have its perfect work, that you may be perfect and complete, lacking in nothing.**" (Jam. 1:2-4) So we should go through temptations.

At first, this would seem to contradict The Lord's Prayer.

"**Bring us not into temptation, but deliver us from the evil one. …**" (Mt. 6:13)

"**… Bring us not into temptation, But deliver us from the evil one.**" (Luke 11:4)

"**… Pray that you don't enter into temptation.**" (Luk. 22:40)

"And said to them, 'Why do you sleep? Rise and pray that you may not enter into temptation.'" (Luk. 22:46)

I think this mean not that we will not experience temptations, but rather that we should not fall into a temptation when we experience it. Another possible interpretation is that the purpose of temptations is to overcome what is here called "the evil one" (or evil in general). If there is another way to deliver us from the evil one, then there is no reason to go through temptations. So this prayer is for us to go through a better way than the way of temptations.

"Watch and pray, that you don't enter into temptation. The spirit indeed is willing, but the flesh is weak." (Mt. 26:41)

"Watch and pray, that you may not enter into temptation. The spirit indeed is willing, but the flesh is weak." (Mrk. 14:38)

The spirit is willing to try a temptation through our flesh, but we should pray for a better way to endure than going through temptations.

"Jesus said to his disciples, 'Most assuredly I say to you, a rich man will enter into the Kingdom of Heaven with difficulty. Again I tell you, it is easier for a camel to go through a needle's eye, than for a rich man to enter into the Kingdom of God.' When the disciples heard it, they were exceedingly astonished, saying, 'Who then can be saved?' Looking at them, Jesus said, 'With men this is impossible, but with God all things are possible.'" (Mt. 19:23-26)

"Jesus, seeing that he became very sad, said, 'How hard it is for those who have riches to enter into the Kingdom of God! For it is easier for a camel to enter in through a needle's eye, than for a rich man to enter into the Kingdom of God.' Those who heard it said, 'Then who can be saved?' But he said, 'The things which are impossible with men are possible with God.'" (Luk. 18:24-27)

God wants us to follow into the Kingdom of God with great difficulty (as great as a camel going through a needle's eye) to demonstrate His glory (that with God all things are possible). Thus we need to be rich for God to show His glory over us.

"**Always carrying in the body the putting to death of the Lord Jesus, that the life of Jesus may also be revealed in our body. For we who live are always delivered to death for Jesus' sake, that the life also of Jesus may be revealed in our mortal flesh.**" (2Cor. 4:10-11)

"**Because it has been granted to you on behalf of Christ, not only to believe in him, but also to suffer on his behalf.**" (Phil. 1:29)

"**Now I rejoice in my sufferings for your sake, and fill up on my part that which is lacking of the afflictions of Christ in my flesh for his body's sake, which is the assembly.**" (Col. 1:24)

These principles apply to us like they do to Christ in section "Temptation of Jesus". We fulfill lacking of the afflictions of Christ in our flesh.

Should we sin?

Through sin, grace is glorified as Christ overcomes this sin.

"What shall we say then? Shall we continue in sin, that grace may abound. May it never be! We who died to sin, how could we live in it any longer?" (Rom. 6:1)

So when we sin, grace is increased more. But this does not work if we sin purposely to increase grace:

"For if we sin willfully after we have received the knowledge of the truth, there remains no more a sacrifice for sins, but a certain fearful expectation of judgment, and a fierceness of fire which will devour the adversaries." (Heb. 10:26-27)

Repented sinners will be elevated above angels

We can only be saved by Christ. He who saves us needs to be as great as Christ. But it happens that as Christ saves us, He does even more: He brings us to the heavens and makes us governors in the heavenly places above the angels.

"… Mercy triumphs over judgment." (Jam. 2:13)

"But the free gift isn't like the trespass. For if by the trespass of the one the many died, much more did the grace of God, and the gift by the grace of the one man, Jesus Christ, abound to the many. The gift is not as through one who sinned: for the judgment came by one to condemnation, but the free gift came of many trespasses to justification. For if by the trespass of the one, death reigned through the one; so much more will those who receive the abundance of grace and of the gift of righteousness reign in life through the one, Jesus Christ. So then as through one trespass, all men were condemned; even so through one act of righteousness, all men were justified to life. For as through the one man's disobedience many were made sinners, even so through the obedience of the one will many be made righteous. The law came in besides, that the trespass might abound; but where sin abounded, grace did abound more exceedingly; that as sin reigned in death, even so might grace reign through righteousness to eternal life through Jesus Christ our Lord." (Rom. 5:15-21)

"Don't you know that the saints will judge the world? And if the world is judged by you, are you unworthy to judge the smallest matters." (1Cor. 6:2)

"Don't you know that we will judge angels?..." (1Cor. 6:3)

"For he didn't subject the world to come, whereof we speak, to angels. But one has somewhere testified, saying, "What is man, that you think of him? Or the son of man, that you care for him?" (Hebrews 2:5-6)

"For if the service of condemnation has glory, the service of righteousness exceeds much more in glory." (2Cor. 3:9)

"He has said to me, 'My grace is sufficient for you, for my power is made perfect in weakness.'

Most gladly therefore I will rather glory in my weaknesses, that the power of Christ may rest on me." (2Cor. 12:9)

"**and raised us up with him, and made us to sit with him in the heavenly places in Christ Jesus.**" (Eph. 2:6)

The Greek verbs for "raised" and "made to sit" are in the Aorist, that is past perfect. This means that we are *already* in the heaven. We may not feel it, but our bodies are controlled by our spirits which are in the heaven.

Redemption

"**That he might redeem those who were under the law, that we might receive the adoption of children.**" (Gal. 4:5)

"**Being justified freely by his grace through the redemption that is in Christ Jesus.**" (Rom. 3:24)

"**In whom we have our redemption through his blood, the forgiveness of our trespasses, according to the riches of his grace.**" (Eph. 1:7)

"**... through his own blood, entered in once for all into the Holy Place, having obtained eternal redemption.**" (Heb. 9:12)

"**Knowing that you were redeemed, not with corruptible things, with silver or gold, from the useless way of life handed down from your fathers, but with precious blood, as of a lamb without spot, the blood of Christ.**" (1Pet. 1:18-19)

Redemption is a two-stage process: First Christ purchases us into His slavery and then He sets us free.

"**... You are not your own, for you were bought with a price. Therefore glorify God in your body and in your spirit, which are God's.**" (1Cor. 6:19-20)

"**You will know the truth, and the truth will make you free.**" (Jn. 8:32)

The truth which sets you free is written in my book "End of Gospel." You will want to read that book, because you need to be set free from the slavery of Christ to finish your redemption by Christ.

"**If therefore the Son makes you free, you will be free indeed.**" (Jn. 8:36)

You shall not remain in slavery.

"**You are my friends, if you do whatever I command you. No longer do I call you servants, for the servant doesn't know what his lord does. But I have called you friends, for everything that I heard from my Father, I have made known to you.**" (Jn. 15:14-15)

"**So you are no longer a bondservant, but a son; and if a son, then an heir of God through Christ.**" (Gal. 4:7)

"**Stand firm therefore in the liberty by which Christ has made us free, and don't be entangled again with a yoke of bondage.**" (Gal. 5:1)

"**For you, brothers, were called for freedom…**" (Gal. 5:13)

So Christ first buys us as slaves, but rather than be a cruel taskmaster, his goal is to free us so we do not need to be slaves to either him or sin anymore.

Read my book "End of Gospel" on the topic "how to become free." I hope there is no need to say how important this is for you.

Note also that one of the main topics of the Old Testament is how the Jews go out from slavery into the freedom that comes from God. It is about Christ setting us free from slavery to Himself. We need to interpret this topic in greater detail.

We are above even the apostles of the New Testament if we declare ourselves free. Paul and Peter write about their being a slave of Christ.

"Paul, a servant of Jesus Christ, called to be an apostle, set apart for the gospel of God." (Rom. 1:1)

"Who then is Apollos, and who is Paul, but servants through whom you believed; and each as the Lord gave to him?" (1Cor. 3:5)

"So let a man think of us as Christ's servants…" (1Cor. 4:1)

"**Paul and Timothy, servants of Jesus Christ…**" (Phil. 1:1)

"**James, a servant of God and of the Lord Jesus Christ…**" (Jam. 1:1)

"**Simon Peter, a servant and apostle of Jesus Christ…**" (2Pet. 1:1)

So as we can see, if we obtain our freedom then we can stand above them.

Gospel about itself

After reading and believing my book "[End of Gospel](#)," now that we are freed from the slavery of Gospel, it tells some things about itself.

"**Now we know that whatever things the law says, it speaks to those who are under the law, that every mouth may be closed, and all the world may be brought under the judgment of God. … For through the law comes the knowledge of sin.**" (Rom. 3:19-20)

This means that when we are set free from slavery, what was once our law (that is Gospel) no longer speaks to us; but in the same way the Old Testament spoke to ancient Jews and not us, from now on the Gospel no longer speaks to us. Instead it speaks to others who are yet in slavery. It is God's word, but no longer is it a word to us. Through Gospel we were made to understand which commandments we failed to obey, but our task now is not to blindly attempt to follow the commandments, but keep them inside so that our inner nature follows the commandments of Gospel by itself. "**Even the righteousness of God through faith in Jesus Christ to all and on all those who believe…**" (Rom. 3:22)

The Gospel terminates itself.

"**But now we have been discharged from the law, having died to that in which we were held; so that we serve in newness of the spirit, and not in oldness of the letter.**" (Rom. 7:6)

"**For I, through the law, died to the law, that I might live to God.**" (Gal. 2:19) This means that for us to live for God we must die for the Gospel just as Gospel died (and was resurrected). We need to stop artificially following the commandments out of a sense of duty, but instead change our inward nature to conform to the commandments of Gospel.

Now we should interpret Gospel as it applies to itself (to Gospel).

"Where is the wise? Where is the scribe? Where is the lawyer of this world? Hasn't God made foolish the wisdom of this world." (1Cor. 1:20)

"Let no one deceive himself. If anyone thinks that he is wise among you in this world, let him become a fool, that he may become wise. For the wisdom of this world is foolishness with God. For it is written, 'He has taken the wise in their craftiness.' And again, 'The Lord knows the reasoning of the wise, that it is worthless.'" (1Cor. 3:18-20)

This means that God has made foolishness the wisdom of the interpreters of Gospel.

The "spiritual authority" of the rulers of the world of Gospel is coming to naught.

"... of the rulers of this world, who are coming to nothing" (1Cor. 2:6)

"Then the end comes, when he will deliver up the Kingdom to God, even the Father; when he will have abolished all rule and all authority and power." (1Cor. 15:24)

We do not need to rule but rather be humble. Christ is perfect anarchy (abolishing every rule and all authority and power).

"For, 'He put all things in subjection under his feet. But when he says, 'All things are put in subjection,' it is evident that he is excepted who subjected all things to him." (1Cor. 15:27)

"Having stripped the principalities and the powers, he made a show of them openly, triumphing over them in it." (Col. 2:15)

Can we lose love?

"Love never fails..." (1Cor. 13:8)

But I was afraid. It is well-documented that every few years all of the atoms of our body are replaced with new ones (which we eat and breathe). Just as the water of a river flows out and is replaced with other water, our body is more like a fluid than a stone. I reasoned: Can love flow out of us and not be replenished so that we could lose it, in spite of the fact that it never ceases?

"**For the love of Christ constrains us; because we judge thus, that one died for all, therefore all died.**" (2Cor. 5:14)

This means that we are defined by the love of Christ. If love could flow out of us, but not replaced we would no longer be ourselves, as we are constrained by the love of Christ. So we can't lose the most important part of our personality: the love of Christ and our main idea "that one died for all, therefore all died." This idea is the foundation of our mind. So we can't lose our main idea.

Baptized in the Holy Spirit

Being Baptized in water is not enough to receive the Holy Spirit.

> "Who, when they had come down, prayed for them, that they might receive the Holy Spirit; for as yet he had fallen on none of them. They had only been baptized in the name of Christ Jesus. Then they laid their hands on them, and they received the Holy Spirit. Now when Simon saw that the Holy Spirit was given through the laying on of the apostles' hands..." (Acts 8:15-16)

One needs to have the hands of apostles laid on him after being baptized in water.

Wonders and spiritual gifts

> "When evening came, they brought to him many possessed with demons. He cast out the spirits with a word, and healed all who were sick; that it might be fulfilled which was spoken through Isaiah the prophet, saying: 'He took our infirmities, and bore our diseases.'" (Mt. 8:16-17)

Before my conversion to Christ I was possessed by demons. I don't mean in a metaphorical sense, I was a real maniacal killer. While under the influence of demons I got to the point where I forgot my name, and was unable to read and count. Despite this oppression, I was cured in an instant when I converted to Christ.

How is it that some preachers say there is no longer spiritual healing, no wonders, and no casting out of demons? If that were true, I would be in a psychiatric clinic, unable to know who I was.

If Christ would not have healed me, I would be a maniacal killer and could not be saved.

"Behold, I send forth the promise of my Father on you. But wait in the city of Jerusalem until you are clothed with power from on high." (Luk. 24:49)

"But he said this about the Spirit, which those believing in him were to receive. For the Holy Spirit was not yet given, because Jesus wasn't yet glorified." "Now when the day of Pentecost had come, they were all with one accord in one place. Suddenly there came from the sky a sound like the rushing of a mighty wind, and it filled all the house where they were sitting. Tongues like fire appeared and were distributed to them, and one

sat on each of them. 4 They were all filled with the Holy Spirit, and began to speak with other languages, as the Spirit gave them the ability to speak." (Jn. 7:39 this refers to the event in Acts 2:1-4)

"I will pray to the Father, and he will give you another Counselor, that he may be with you forever,— the Spirit of truth, whom the world can't receive; for it doesn't see him, neither knows him. You know him, for he lives with you, and will be in you." (Jn. 14:16-17)

That it will be with us forever means that wonders will never cease.

Which Bible verse bear witness to the "cessationism" point of view (that is that the wonders ceased at the end of the first century)? I know of no such verse.

There were prophets not only in the Old Testament but also in the time of the New Testament.

"Now in these days, prophets came down from Jerusalem to Antioch." (Act. 11:27)

"Now in the assembly that was at Antioch there were some prophets and teachers: Barnabas, Simeon who was called Niger, Lucius of Cyrene, Manaen the foster-brother of Herod the tetrarch, and Saul." (Act. 13:1)

"Judas and Silas, also being prophets themselves…" (Act. 15:32)

"When Paul had laid his hands on them, the Holy Spirit came on them, and they spoke with other languages and prophesied." (Act. 19:6)

"Now this man had four virgin daughters who prophesied." (Act. 21:9)

"As we stayed there some days, a certain prophet named Agabus came down from Judea." (Act. 21:10)

"Don't neglect the gift that is in you, which was given to you by prophecy…" (1Tim. 4:14)

"Follow after love, and earnestly desire spiritual gifts, but especially that you may prophesy." (1Cor. 14:1)

These verses clearly tell us that even if we have love, it is not enough. We also need other spiritual gifts, especially prophecy.

"Now I desire to have you all speak with other languages, but rather that you would prophesy. For he is greater who prophesies than he who speaks with other languages, unless he interprets, that the assembly may be built up." (1Cor. 14:5)

"But if all prophesy, and someone unbelieving or unlearned comes in, he is reproved by all, and he is judged by all. And thus the secrets of his heart are revealed. So he will fall down on his face and worship God, declaring that God is among you indeed." (1Cor. 14:24-25)

We are to also desire for every one of us to speak in tongues. Paul spoke in tongues more than the members of the Corinthian church, and he called us to follow his example.

"I thank my God, I speak with other languages more than you all." (1Cor. 14:18)

My computer fan roared loudly, disturbing me to write this book. For some reason this happens after I switch on my computer after it has been turned off for an extended period of time. After a period of time it quiets down. This is not a huge problem since I usually don't turn the computer off. It just so happened that I touched the computer because I was annoyed with the noise. The moment I touched it, it stopped roaring. Was this a coincidence, or did I, not knowing I was filled with Holy Spirit "heal" the computer? No doubt, if I were to have been filled with the Holy Spirit to a greater degree, He could have made me able to work despite the noise. But it did happen, the question is what happened.

Chapter 7   Reincarnation

Most Christian teachers teach that there is no such thing as reincarnation (as in Hinduism and Buddhism).

But the Bible says that the spirit of one man may come into another.

"Yahweh came down in the cloud, and spoke to him, and took of the Spirit that was on him, and put it on the seventy elders: and it happened that when the Spirit rested on them, they prophesied, but they did so no more." (Num. 11:25)

So the spirit of Moses came upon 70 other people. It can be called reincarnation. Likewise the spirit of Elijah has come onto Elisha (2Kin. 2).

This sometimes may take the form of a classic "reincarnation" where one person remembers the life of another dead person through the spirit.

Jesus said speaking of John the Baptizer, **"If you are willing to receive it, this is Elijah, who is to come."** (Mt. 11:14)

This means that John was a reincarnation of Elijah for those people willing to believe that he was Elijah, but not for those unwilling to accept the spirit of Elijah. That is, the first category of people speaking with John would have heard Elijah, but the second group would not.

"**But I tell you that Elijah has come already, and they didn't recognize him, but did to him whatever they wanted to… Then the disciples understood that he spoke to them of John the Baptizer.**" (Mt. 17:12-13)

"**He said to them, 'Elijah indeed comes first, and restores all things. How is it written about the Son of Man, that he should suffer many things and be despised? But I tell you that Elijah has come, and they have also done to him whatever they wanted to, even as it is written about him.'**" (Mrk. 9:12-13)

"**He will go before him in the spirit and power of Elijah…**" (Luk. 1:17)

Chapter 8 Interpretation of Bible

"**You search the Scriptures, because you think that in them you have eternal life; and these are they which testify about me.**" (Jn. 5:39)

Everything in the Bible should be interpreted as a revealing a truth about Christ Jesus.

"**For it is written in the law of Moses, "You shall not muzzle an ox while it treads out the grain." Is it for the oxen that God cares, or does he say it assuredly for our sake? Yes, it was written for our sake, because he who plows ought to plow in hope, and he who threshes in hope should partake of his hope.**" (1Cor. 9:9)

This clearly reveals that the Old Testament contains so-called spiritual sense. It says much about oxen and other animals, but this also has a spiritual sense that can help us.

"Now these things were our examples, to the intent we should not lust after evil things, as they also lusted." (1Cor. 10:6)

"Now all these things happened to them by way of example, and they were written for our admonition, on whom the ends of the ages have come." (1Cor. 10:11)

According to this verse the Old Testament was written in order to be a teaching example for *us*.

The following interpretation would be proclaimed incorrect by many theologians.

"Now the promises were spoken to Abraham and to his seed. He doesn't say, 'To seeds,' as of many, but as of one, 'To your seed,' which is Christ." (Gal. 3:16) The theologians would say "The word *seed* may mean a progenitor or progenitors according to our dictionaries, but in this context it means *progenitors* as is clear from the context." But no, the Bible means what is says and should be taken literally, not based on man's interpretation or what it seems to mean.

Don't follow every example in Bible. For example, you should not follow after the biblical example of Cain. **"Woe to them! For they went in the way of Cain, and ran riotously in the error of Balaam for hire, and perished in Korah's rebellion."** (Jud. 1:11)

Chapter 9 Prosperity Gospel

Many Bible verses confirm the teaching of Prosperity Gospel (see some verses below). Indeed, they are so prevalent that one would have to be blind not to see them.

"**Don't lay up treasures for yourselves on the earth, where moth and rust consume, and where thieves break through and steal; but lay up for yourselves treasures in heaven, where neither moth nor rust consume, and where thieves don't break through and steal;**" (Mt. 6:19-20)

It is clear that by taking advantage of good deals (not just deals but deals of faith) we can lay up a personal treasure in heaven where there are no bank robbers.

But it is less clear that you can use the riches of heavens here on Earth. This is like depositing money into a bank. You can lay something there and get more back than you put in.

"And tasted the good word of God, and the powers of the age to come." (Heb. 6:5)

So it is now clear that Mt. 6:19-20 is calling you to store your treasure in heaven instead of using a bank on the Earth.

"No one can serve two masters, for either he will hate the one and love the other; or else he will be devoted to one and despise the other. You can't serve both God and Mammon." (Mt. 6:24)

To serve Mammon means attempting to get rich using the means of this world (a common commercial business not based on faith or worse, cheating) rather than faith, charity, and good deals. Your money is either stored in heaven by God or you belong to this world system (Mammon).

"Therefore, I tell you, don't be anxious for your life: what you will eat, or what you will drink; nor yet for your body, what you will wear. Isn't life more than food, and the body more than clothing?" (Mt. 6:25)

"Therefore don't be anxious, saying, 'What will we eat?', 'What will we drink?' or, 'With what will we be clothed?' For the Gentiles seek after all these things, for your heavenly Father knows that you need all these things. But seek first God's Kingdom, and his righteousness; and all these things will be given to you as well." (Mt. 6:31-33)

"He said to his disciples, 'Therefore I tell you, don't be anxious for your life, what you will eat, nor yet for your body, what you will wear. Life is more than food, and the body is more than clothing.'" (Luk. 12:22-23)

Our human logic is the exact opposite of the logic of Jesus. Human logic causes us to suppose that since our life is important we should be worried about what to eat and drink in order to preserve our life. But Jesus tells to concentrate on more important things through the faith and if we do so God will provide the less important but critical things (food, drink, clothes) that support our life. If we seek first God's Kingdom and his righteousness, we will have "all these things" (food, drink, clothes).

"...Jesus answered her, 'Martha, Martha, you are anxious and troubled about many things, but one thing is needed. Mary has chosen the good part, which will not be taken away from her.'" (Luk. 10:38-42)

"Come to me, all you who labor and are heavily burdened, and I will give you rest… will find rest for your souls. For my yoke is easy, and my burden is light." (Mt. 11:28-30)

It may mean that Christ will give those who come to Him in prayer enough money to have rest and not work all the time.

It looks like capitalism is wrong. These who have money earn even more with little or no work, and these who don't have money earn less and less with greater difficulties. But rest assured that things even out in heaven.

"For whoever has, to him will be given, and he will have abundance, but whoever doesn't have, from him will be taken away even that which he has." (Mt. 13:12)

"**For to everyone who has will be given, and he will have abundance, but from him who has not, even that which he has will be taken away.**" (Mt. 25:29)

"**For whoever has, to him will more be given, and he who doesn't have, from him will be taken away even that which he has.**" (Mrk. 4:25)

"**… whoever has, to him will be given; and whoever doesn't have, from him will be taken away even that which he thinks he has.**" (Luk. 8:18) "**For I tell you that to everyone who has, will more be given; but from him who doesn't have, even that which he has will be taken away from him.**" (Luk. 19:26)

So despite all of the deficiencies of capitalism, we can hardly devise a better economic system, as this is God's economic model in heaven. That being said, God calls us to strive for equality:

"**For this is not that others may be eased and you distressed, but for equality. Your abundance at this present time supplies their lack, that their**

abundance also may become a supply for your lack; that there may be equality. As it is written, 'He who gathered much had nothing left over, and he who gathered little had no lack.'" (2Cor. 8:13-15)

"Again, the Kingdom of Heaven is like a treasure hidden in the field, which a man found, and hid. In his joy, he goes and sells all that he has, and buys that field." (Mt. 13:44)

This probably means that we should invest all of our resources into a Christian ministry, selling all business investments which we may have.

"Again, the Kingdom of Heaven is like a man who is a merchant seeking fine pearls, who having found one pearl of great price, he went and sold all that he had, and bought it." (Mt. 13:45-46)

This means that in the Kingdom of Heaven when we find things which are exceedingly more important than other good things, we need to concentrate on that one particular task, abandoning all others.

"For the Son of Man will come in the glory of his Father with his angels, and then he will render to everyone according to his deeds." (Mt. 16:27)

Note that in the end we will receive according to our own deeds, not according to how much we donated to others (however a donation is also a deed).

"Give, and it will be given to you…" (Luk. 6:38)

It is quite clear that if you give away money, then money will be given to you.

"So is he who lays up treasure for himself, and is not rich toward God." (Luk. 12:21)

I'd better translate "rich into God." This means that our riches can be put into God just like they can be deposited into a bank.

"Sell that which you have, and give gifts to the needy. Make for yourselves purses which don't grow old, a treasure in the heavens that doesn't fail, where no thief approaches, neither moth destroys." (Luk. 12:33)

By giving gifts to the needy we store money in "God's bank" in heaven. Then we can request the money in the prayer back.

"Jesus said to them, '… He who comes to me will not be hungry, and he who believes in me will never be thirsty.'" (Jn. 6:35)

Jesus does not lie. Whoever has the proper faith will never be hungry or thirsty. The need will be met through money or some other way.

"I am the door. If anyone enters in by me, he will be saved, and will go in and go out, and will find pasture." (Jn. 10:9)

We know that whoever enters through Christ is saved, but he will also find "pasture" which apparently means material goods.

"Beloved, I pray that you may prosper in all things and be healthy, even as your soul prospers." (3Jn. 1:2)

"So then, those who are of faith are blessed with the faithful Abraham." (Gal. 3:9)

The word "blessed" translated literally means "rich."

The following is weird:

"**… people of corrupt minds and destitute of the truth, who suppose that godliness is a means of gain. Withdraw yourself from such.**" (1Tim. 6:5)

Isn't godliness a means for community gain (not personal gain)? Did I misunderstand something?

Was Jesus rich?

I do not agree with some preachers who claim that Jesus was a really rich person in the sense of this world.

"**Jesus said to him, 'The foxes have holes, and the birds of the sky have nests, but the Son of Man has nowhere to lay his head.'**" (Mt. 8:20)

"**Jesus said to him, 'The foxes have holes, and the birds of the sky have nests, but the Son of Man has no place to lay his head.'**" (Luk. 9:58)

But surely He was not very poor for soon after his birth He received some treasures (so these became His property) (Mt. 2:11)

"… Opening their treasures, they offered to him gifts: gold, frankincense, and myrrh."

While these were great riches during Bible times, it seems there were times when there was not enough money available to meet their everyday needs. Because of this God needed to miraculously provide.

"But, lest we cause them to stumble, go to the sea, and cast a hook, and take up the first fish that comes up. When you have opened its mouth, you will find a stater coin. Take that, and give it to them for me and you." (Mt. 17:27)

Other

"Blessed are the poor by spirit, For theirs is the Kingdom of Heaven." (Mt. 5:3, modified translation)

This is about people who were filled by and controlled by the spirit so much that they didn't need money. This does not mean that you give away all of your money and begin to live in poverty, because that would amount to being poor by letter rather than by spirit and that is not what Jesus is referring to. From this verse we know that being blessed with money isn't obligatory, there are people who may efficiently live without it. However that verse can also be understood another way: "Blessed are the beggars of spirit." That is, those who repeatedly ask God to give them more of his spirit.

Finally, God will pay us by the *works* we have done, not just by our donations to others.

"Who 'will pay back to everyone according to their works'" (Rom. 2:6)

"… each will receive his own reward according to his own labor." (1Cor. 3:8)

"… I will give to each one of you according to your deeds" (Rev. 2:23)

"Behold, I come quickly. My reward is with me, to repay to each man according to his work." (Rev. 22:12)

"For the love of money is a root of all kinds of evil…" (1Tim. 6:10)

I conclude that if people were not so greedy they would have contact with aliens (who don't want to deal with people, for why would they want to be in contact with those who would destroy the heavenly economy by their greed) and this would help to wipe out all kinds of evil.

"And if a brother or sister is naked and in lack of daily food, and one of you tells them, 'Go in peace, be warmed and filled;' and yet you didn't give them the things the body needs, what good is it?" (James 2:15-16)

"But whoever has the world's goods, and sees his brother in need, and closes his heart of compassion against him, how does the love of God remain in him? My little children, let's not love in word only, neither with the tongue only, but in deed and truth." (1Jn. 3:17-18)

But some of us say "we will help your poverty by offering up a prayer." No, not just a prayer, you should also be willing to give away your money.

Some preachers strive to use the blood of Christ as if it were something common, for common needs. It is precious and should be used sparingly:

"But with precious blood, as of a lamb without spot, the blood of Christ." (1Pet. 1:19)

Chapter 10   Miscellaneous

"**Now the birth of Jesus Christ was like this; for after his mother, Mary, was engaged to Joseph, before they came together, she was found pregnant by the Holy Spirit.**" (Mt. 1:18)

From the words "before they came together" it seems that Joseph was not impotent because of age, as some (notably Catholics) suppose. The Bible makes this plain in other passages and even goes on to say that Mary had other children.

"**And didn't know her sexually until she had brought forth her firstborn son. He named him Jesus.**" (Mt. 1:25)

"**Isn't this the carpenter's son? Isn't his mother called Mary, and his brothers, James, Joses, Simon, and Judas? Aren't all of his sisters with us?...**" (Mt. 13:55-56)

"Isn't this the carpenter, the son of Mary, and brother of James, Joses, Judas, and Simon? Aren't his sisters here with us? ..." (Mrk. 6:3)

"For even his brothers didn't believe in him." (Jn. 7:5)

"... brothers of the Lord..." (1Cor. 9:5)

"... except James, the Lord's brother." (Gal. 1:19)

"... an angel of the Lord appeared to him in a dream, saying, "Joseph, son of David, don't be afraid to take to yourself Mary, your wife, for that which is conceived in her is of the Holy Spirit. She shall bring forth a son. You shall call his name Jesus, for it is he who shall save his people from their sins." (Mt. 1:20-21)

See also Mt. 12:13, 19, 22. Thus prophetic dreams really exist and are not a human fantasy. However, I don't believe in books that talk about specific methods for interpreting individual objects in dreams.

"In those days, John the Baptizer came, preaching in the wilderness of Judea, saying, 'Repent, for the Kingdom of Heaven is at hand!'" (Mt. 3:1, 2)

"From that time, Jesus began to preach, and to say, 'Repent! For the Kingdom of Heaven is at hand.'" (Mt. 4:17)

"As you go, preach, saying, 'The Kingdom of Heaven is at hand!'" (Mt. 10:7)

It sounds quite awesome in modern language: "The Space Empire has come!"

"Jerusalem, Jerusalem, who kills the prophets, and stones those who are sent to her! How often would I have gathered your children together, even as a hen gathers her chickens under her wings, and you would not!" (Mt. 23:37)

"Jerusalem, Jerusalem, that kills the prophets, and stones those who are sent to her! How often I wanted to gather your children together, like a hen gathers her own brood under her wings, and you refused." (Luk. 13:34)

The "wings" of Christ are His spaceships, He wants to gather us with His spaceships.

"Then the devil took him into the holy city. He set him on the pinnacle of the temple, and said to him, 'If you are the Son of God, throw yourself down, for it is written, "He will give his angels charge concerning you." and, "On their hands they will bear you up, So that you don't dash your foot against a stone."' Jesus said to him, "Again, it is written, 'You shall not test the Lord, your God.'"" (Mt. 4:5-7)

A similar passage is found in Luke 4:9-12. This means that we should not ignore natural laws such as the laws of physics, biology, or social processes when we set our hope on God; otherwise Jesus would have ignored the law of gravity and jump.

"Blessed are those who mourn, For they shall be comforted." (Mt. 5:4)

Compare these verses from the Old Testament.

"A good name is better than fine perfume; and the day of death better than the day of one's birth.

It is better to go to the house of mourning than to go to the house of feasting: for that is the end of all men, and the living should take this to heart. Sorrow is better than laughter; for by the sadness of the face the heart is made good. The heart of the wise is in the house of mourning; but the heart of fools is in the house of mirth." (Ecc. 7:1-4)

"Lament, mourn, and weep. Let your laughter be turned to mourning, and your joy to gloom." (Jam. 4:9)

Thus these churches which spend all their time rejoicing in their meetings are not following the best way.

"Blessed are the gentle, For they shall inherit the earth." (Mt. 5:5)

Saved people will inherit plots in the heavens. However those who are gentle will receive a special blessing (among the heavenly blessings), plots of land on Earth.

"Give to him who asks you, and don't turn away him who desires to borrow from you." (Mt. 5:42)

"Give to everyone who asks you, and don't ask him who takes away your goods to give them back again." (Luk. 6:30)

Apparently, this means that you should give away whatever someone asks for. But a more careful reading of this verse means that you shall give only to someone who asks *you*. This means that you should give to somebody anything they ask, *only* if they understand who you are, what kind of person you are, what you believe in, etc.

"That you may be children of your Father who is in heaven. For he makes his sun to rise on the evil and the good, and sends rain on the just and the unjust." (Mt. 5:45)

Note that the sun belongs to God and is His property. Why then do some preachers say that the sun is controlled by the Devil?

"Moreover when you fast, don't be like the hypocrites, with sad faces. For they disfigure their faces, that they may be seen by men to be fasting. Most assuredly I tell you, they have received their reward." (Mt. 6:16)

Note that Christ doesn't say "don't be hypocrites" but "don't be like the hypocrites." This means that not only should we not be hypocrites, we should strive to not even be like hypocrites. Note what hypocrites do and do otherwise.

"Therefore don't be anxious for tomorrow, for tomorrow will be anxious for itself. Each day's own evil is sufficient." (Mt. 6:34)

Jesus isn't saying not to do long-term planning or not to plan your next day. He is just saying we should not to be anxious for tomorrow. As I understand, the word "anxious" here means to worry about small things (such as food, drink, etc.) but instead engage in long-term planning of the important things.

"**Therefore whatever you desire for men to do to you, you shall also do to them; for this is the law and the prophets.**" (Mt. 7:12)

This golden rule is the main principle of the Old Testament. Anything in the Old Testament are special cases of this principle. Note that the principle of the New Testament is something else.

"**Jesus said to him, 'You shall love the Lord your God with all your heart, and with all your soul, and with all your mind.' This is the first and great commandment. A second likewise is this, 'You shall love your neighbor as yourself.' The whole law and the prophets depend on these two commandments.'**" (Mt. 22:37-40)

"**For the whole law is fulfilled in one word, in this: 'You shall love your neighbor as yourself.'**" (Gal. 5:14)

"**Behold, a leper came to him and worshiped him, saying, 'Lord, if you want to, you can make me clean.' Jesus stretched out his hand, and**

touched him, saying, 'I want to. Be made clean.' Immediately his leprosy was cleansed." (Mt. 8:2-3)

"There came to him a leper, begging him, kneeling down to him, and saying to him, 'If you want to, you can make me clean.' Being moved with compassion, he stretched out his hand, and touched him, and said to him, 'I want to. Be made clean.' When he had said this, immediately the leprosy departed from him, and he was made clean." (Mrk. 1:40-42)

Note that in the Old Testament it was a sin to even touch leprous people, but for Jesus there was an exception because His touching cured (and so when He touched the man he was no more leprous).

"… for there is nothing covered that will not be revealed; and hidden that will not be known" (Mt. 10:26)

"For nothing is hidden, that will not be revealed; nor anything secret, that will not be known and come to light." (Luk. 8:17)

"**But there is nothing covered up, that will not be revealed, nor hidden, that will not be known.**" (Luk. 12:2)

For many years it seemed that some things were lost forever such as ships that sunk in the deepest part of the Ocean. But now we have new technologies and are able to raise things from the bottom of the sea, do a DNA analysis and so on, revealing previously lost things. Just like in the Kingdom of Heaven, anything covered will be revealed.

"**I thank you, Father, Lord of heaven and earth**" (Mt. 11:25)

"**Jesus came to them and spoke to them, saying, 'All authority has been given to me in heaven and on earth.'**" (Mt. 28:18)

"**For 'the earth is the Lord's, and its fullness.'**" (1Cor. 10:26)

This means that not only the heavens but the Earth is all God's possession, in spite of the sins of the people.

"Even as the Son of Man came not to be served, but to serve, and to give his life as a ransom for many." (Mt. 20:28)

"For the Son of Man also came not to be served, but to serve, and to give his life as a ransom for many." (Mrk. 10:45)

This does mean that the reason Christ came was not so that we would serve Him in our Sunday church meetings. His reason was another: to serve us.

"You will hear of wars and rumors of wars. See that you aren't troubled, for all this must happen, but the end is not yet." (Mt. 24:6)

"Rumors of war" means rumors in the sense of a psychological weapon. In modern language this is called an "informational war." See also Mrk. 13:7.

"The beginning of the gospel of Jesus Christ, the Son of God." (Mrk. 1:1)

It seems from this verse that the Gospel of Matthew is placed in the beginning of the New

Testament by mistake, it should be the Gospel of Mark instead.

Wasn't man created to serve the Lord as in Sunday (or Saturday, dependently on your denomination)? No: "**He said to them, 'The Sabbath was made for man, not man for the Sabbath.'**" (Mrk. 2:27)

About Mary, the mother of Jesus:

"**Yes, a sword will pierce through your own soul, that the thoughts of many hearts may be revealed.**" (Luk. 2:35)

This suggests that Mary possessed the gift of telepathy, so that through her the thoughts of people were revealed. St. Paul also had this gift:

"**For though I am absent in the flesh, yet am I with you in the spirit, rejoicing and seeing your order, and the steadfastness of your faith in Christ.**" (Col. 2:5)

"**The devil, leading him up on a high mountain, showed him all the kingdoms of the world in a moment of time.**" (Luk. 4:5) This shows that the devil is a very powerful computer, as he can show a great deal of information so quickly.

"… But to whom little is forgiven, the same loves little." (Luk. 7:47)

I suppose that angels, which are almost righteous and for whom little is therefore forgiven, don't love much. This is the reason that saints who are repented sinners will be above angels in the world to come.

"Behold, I give you authority to tread on serpents and scorpions, and over all the power of the enemy. Nothing will in any way hurt you." (Luk. 10:19)

Some living things (serpents, scorpions, and so on) were created by Devil.

"then the lord of that servant will come in a day when he isn't expecting him, and in an hour that he doesn't know, and will cut him in two, and place his portion with the unfaithful" (Luk. 12:46)

This may mean that as a form of punishment the Lord will split the personality of bad servants into two parts (probably splitting into the left and right hemispheres of the brain similar to a lobotomy, or into the conscious or unconscious parts).

"**A certain one of them struck the servant of the high priest, and cut off his right ear. But Jesus answered, 'Let me at least do this'—and he touched his ear, and healed him.**" (Luk. 22:50-51)

Does this mean that Jesus caused his ear to grow again or did he just heal the wound? I don't know.

"**It is the spirit who gives life. The flesh profits nothing. The words that I speak to you are spirit, and are life.**" (Jn. 6:63)

We are flesh not spirit. We should be astonished to hear that there is nothing of value in our lives. But Jesus immediately follows this up by saying that His words are spirit. So, despite our being flesh, there is something useful inside of us, His words, which we hear. So we are not entirely useless.

"**I have other sheep, which are not of this fold. I must bring them also, and they will hear my voice.**

They will become one flock with one shepherd." (Jn. 10:16)

Traditionally this verse is explained as referring to gentiles who will become one flock with the Jews. But is Christ talking about aliens from other planets? (or maybe some spirits in the heaven, which would be made one flock with us?)

"... The words that I tell you, I speak not from myself; but the Father who lives in me does his works." (Jn. 14:10)

"... The word which you hear isn't mine, but the Father's who sent me." (Jn. 14:24)

Jesus spoke not what He desired to say, but by a prepared pattern. See my book "[End of Gospel](#)".

"They were all filled with the Holy Spirit, and began to speak with other languages, as the Spirit gave them the ability to speak. Now there were dwelling in Jerusalem Jews, devout men, from every nation under the sky. When this sound was heard, the multitude came together, and were bewildered, because everyone heard them

speaking in his own language. They were all amazed and marveled, saying to one another, "Behold, aren't all these who speak Galileans? How do we hear, everyone in our own native language? Parthians, Medes, Elamites, and people from Mesopotamia, Judea, Cappadocia, Pontus, Asia, Phrygia, Pamphylia, Egypt, the parts of Libya around Cyrene, visitors from Rome, both Jews and proselytes, Cretans and Arabians: we hear them speaking in our languages the mighty works of God!" They were all amazed, and were perplexed, saying one to another, 'What does this mean?" (Act. 2:4-12)

I think this means that they all *simultaneously* spoke in several languages at once. By the great wisdom of the Holy Spirit the grammar of the languages was arranged in such a way that one phrase was meaningful in several languages at once.

"As he traveled, it happened that he got close to Damascus, and suddenly a light from the sky shone around him. He fell on the earth, and heard a voice saying to him, 'Saul, Saul, why do you

persecute me?' He said, 'Who are you, Lord?' The Lord said, 'I am Jesus, whom you are persecuting. But rise up, and enter into the city, and you will be told what you must do.'" (Act. 9:3-6)

It seems that after having heard the words "Saul, Saul, why do you persecute me?" that Saul guessed it was Jesus speaking to him. This was the reason he asked "Who are you, Lord?"

"Let every soul be in subjection to the higher authorities, for there is no authority except from God, and those who exist are ordained by God. Therefore he who resists the authority, withstands the ordinance of God; and those who withstand will receive to themselves judgment." (Rom. 13:1-2)

This is also about spiritual authorities. We should not make war with ruling spirits.

"Now may the God of hope fill you with all joy and peace in believing, that you may abound in hope, in the power of the Holy Spirit." (Rom. 15:13)

I translate it as *dream* rather than *hope*. So we should "abound in dreams" and dream much in the power of the Holy Spirit, who is able to fulfill our dreams.

"**each man's work will be revealed. For the Day will declare it, because it is revealed in fire; and the fire itself will test what sort of work each man's work is. If any man's work remains which he built on it, he will receive a reward. If any man's work is burned, he will suffer loss, but he himself will be saved, but as through fire.**" (1Cor. 3:13-15)

I think, "fire" refers to the comet which will fall upon the Earth (see chapter Chapter 11). If your works remain after the comet sets the Earth on fire, you will receive a reward. If it burns, you will lose your reward.

Some people thought: Why not destroy our own bodies (be it with suicide or sinful living), since only the spiritual ones are important. God has an answer to this. "**Don't you know that you are a temple of**

God, and that God's Spirit lives in you? If anyone destroys the temple of God, God will destroy him; for God's temple is holy, which you are." (1Cor. 3:16-17)

The very reason the Holy Spirit entered into us is to cure us because we are sinners. Since a member of the Trinity is living inside of us that means we are His holy temple; and no one has the right to destroy or harm God's holy temple.

"For the Kingdom of God is not in word, but in power." (1Cor. 4:20)

It is natural to imagine that the heavenly Kingdom of God consists of knowing mysteries ("words"), but it is instead having more energy.

"are to deliver such a one to Satan for the destruction of the flesh, that the spirit may be saved in the day of the Lord Jesus." (1Cor. 5:5)

"of whom is Hymenaeus and Alexander; whom I delivered to Satan, that they might be taught not to blaspheme." (1Tim. 1:20)

So the task of Satan is not just directly opposite of the task of God and our task. Satan destroys the body, not spirit as we might think.

It is natural to suppose that different spiritual services are done with different spirits. But this is wrong: See 1Cor. 12:5-11.

"… **Do all speak with various languages?…**" (1Cor. 12:30)

From this verse I conclude that the Pentecostal teaching that everybody baptized by the Holy Spirit will speak in tongues is wrong.

"**But the day of the Lord will come as a thief in the night; in which the heavens will pass away with a great noise, and the elements will be dissolved with fervent heat, and the earth and the works that are in it will be burned up. Therefore since all these things are thus to be destroyed, what manner of persons ought you to be in holy living and godliness, looking for and earnestly desiring the coming of the day of God, by reason of which the heavens being on fire will be**

dissolved, and the elements will melt with fervent heat?" (2Pet. 3:10-12)

Once the Universe is burned, what remains of it?

"But now faith, hope, and love remain—these three…" (1Cor. 13:13)

These are the non-flammable things. It is what remains of us when we die. Our faith, hope, and love continue to exist after our death. Thus we continue in eternal life.

We are sinners, able to do almost nothing, but in us there is the Spirit. One task which we nevertheless are able to do in our flesh is to travel to some location. It is enough for the Spirit to do a work through us.

"For though we walk in the flesh, we don't wage war according to the flesh; for the weapons of our warfare are not of the flesh, but mighty before God to the throwing down of strongholds, throwing down imaginations and every high thing that is exalted against the knowledge of God, and bringing every thought into captivity to the

obedience of Christ; and being in readiness to avenge all disobedience, when your obedience will be made full." (2Cor. 10:3-6)

"But I counted it necessary to send to you Epaphroditus, my brother, fellow worker, fellow soldier, and your apostle and minister to my need." (Phil. 2:25)

Note that the apostle Epaphroditus was not one of the twelve and neither was Paul. So there are more apostles than just the original twelve and Paul.

"I charge you before God, who gives life to all things, and before Christ Jesus, who before Pontius Pilate testified the good confession." (1Tim. 6:13)

How can giving life to all things and testifying a good confession before Pontius Pilate be compared? The answer is that testifying a good confession before Pontius Pilate is comparably as difficult as giving life to all things. It is very hard to say something sensible when you are before the unjust court of such an evil man.

"which in its own times he will show, who is the blessed and only Ruler, the King of kings, and Lord of lords; who alone has immortality, dwelling in unapproachable light; whom no man has seen, nor can see: to whom be honor and eternal power. Amen." (1Tim. 6:15-16)

He *has* immortality, we *rent* immortality from Him.

It is a wrong teaching that if somebody is an apostle then he cannot be also a teacher (or a pastor, or whatever).

"… I was appointed as a preacher, an apostle, and a teacher of the Gentiles." (2Tim. 1:11)

St. Paul was *both* an apostle and a teacher.

Note that Jesus himself is also called an apostle:

"… consider the Apostle and High Priest of our confession, Jesus." (Heb. 3:1)

"For this they willfully forget, that there were heavens from of old, and an earth formed out of

water and amid water, by the word of God." (2Pet. 3:5)

I suspect that here the word *water* should mean *hydrogen* (one of the components of water). Astronomy and astrophysics confirm that this world was made out of hydrogen.

"**... Freely you received, so freely give.**" (Mt. 10:8) These words of Jesus were fulfilled by Richard Stallman (even though he is an atheist), who developed GPL (GNU General Public License), the license of software where every modification to freely received software should also be free. It is a commandment of Jesus to use licenses such as GPL. Examples of software with this license include Linux. Jesus wants us to become Linux users.

"**The stars of the sky fell to the earth, like a fig tree dropping its unripe figs when it is shaken by a great wind.**" (Rev. 6:13)

Certainly stars cannot fall onto the Earth. I understand this verse as referring to the spirits of stars who fall onto the Earth.

"**... God, who gives life to all things.**" (1Tim. 6:13)

"All things" includes stones, wooden beams, and furniture. When God is near, everything becomes alive.

Soul

How to reconcile the Christian doctrine of the soul and the scientific fact that a human thinks with his brain? My resolution is the following: A human thinks with his brain but the soul is a warranty for the body and a backup for the brain. This is a quite natural theory: God created people as agricultural robots "**... a man to till the ground**" (Gen. 2:5) and created us with an eternal warranty and backup.

The Bible says that branding the head with a hot iron can damage the conscious.

"**through the hypocrisy of men who speak lies, branded in their own conscience as with a hot iron.**" (1Tim. 4:2) Thus a man is ruled by the brain according to the Bible.

The Apocalypse confirms that the souls of people have a mind and conscience even after death:

"**When he opened the fifth seal, I saw underneath the altar the souls of those who had been killed for the Word of God, and for the testimony of the Lamb which they had. They cried with a loud voice, saying, "How long, Master, the holy and true, until you judge and avenge our blood on those who dwell on the earth?" A long white robe was given to each of them. They were told that they should rest yet for a while, until their fellow servants and their brothers, who would also be killed even as they were, should complete their course.**" (Rev. 6:9-11)

Seeming contradictions in Gospel

"**Now when Jesus was born in Bethlehem of Judea in the days of Herod the king…**" (Mt. 2:1)

Note that there were several kings with the name Herod. Thus the "contradictions" in Gospel proposed by some Gospel critics about Herod are the result of a misunderstanding.

"…, for most assuredly I tell you, you will not have gone through the cities of Israel, until the Son of Man has come." (Mt. 10:23)

This statement of Jesus seems erroneous. A possible explanation is Mt. 17:1-3 (see below).

Those such as the Jehovah's Witnesses who don't believe in the divinity of Christ have no biblical arguments to support their belief except two verses where Jesus says that He does not know something:

"But no one knows of that day and hour, not even the angels of heaven, but my Father only." (Mt. 24:36)

"But of that day or that hour no one knows, not even the angels in heaven, nor the Son, but only the Father." (Mrk. 13:32)

These verses are a very strong argument against the supreme divinity of Christ, but I will try to interpret it in such a way that brings it into agreement with other verses that proclaim the divinity of Christ.

"All things have been delivered to me by my Father. No one knows the Son, except the Father; neither does anyone know the Father, except the Son, and he to whom the Son desires to reveal him." (Mt. 11:27)

Note that as no one knows the Son except the Father, the Son does not know himself. This means that (ahead of time) Christ does not know which decisions He himself will make. Since Christ will decide the day of His coming, He does not know His own decision ahead of time. Christ knows everything, but does not know himself.

"Most assuredly I tell you, there are some standing here who will in no way taste of death, until they see the Son of Man coming in his kingdom." (Mt. 16:28)

This seems false, as the twelve apostles died before the second coming of Christ. But you will understand this if you read the next chapter of Gospel:

"**After six days, Jesus took with him Peter, James, and John his brother, and brought them up into a high mountain by themselves. He was transfigured before them. His face shone like the sun, and his garments became as white as the light. Behold, Moses and Elijah appeared to them talking with him.**" (Mt. 17:1-3)

So they saw the Son of Man coming in his kingdom. The same thing is recorded in the Gospel of Mark.

"**He said to them, 'Most assuredly I tell you, there are some standing here who will in no way taste death until they see the Kingdom of God come with power.' After six days Jesus took with him Peter, James, and John, and brought them up onto a high mountain privately by themselves, and he was changed into another form in front of them. His clothing became glistening, exceedingly white, like snow, such as no launderer on earth** can whiten them. Elijah and Moses appeared to them, and they were talking with Jesus." (Mrk. 9:1-4)

The Gospel of Luke confirms these events.

"'But I tell you the truth: There are some of those who stand here, who will in no way taste of death, until they see the Kingdom of God.' It happened about eight days after these sayings, that he took with him Peter, John, and James, and went up onto the mountain to pray. As he was praying, the appearance of his face was altered, and his clothing became white and dazzling. Behold, two men were talking with him, who were Moses and Elijah, who appeared in glory, and spoke of his departure, which he was about to accomplish at Jerusalem. Now Peter and those who were with him were heavy with sleep, but when they were fully awake, they saw his glory, and the two men who stood with him." (Luk. 9:27-31)

Words of people

Regarding Saul's meeting with Jesus Christ in glory:

"The men who traveled with him stood speechless, hearing the sound, but seeing no one." (Act. 9:7)

"Those who were with me indeed saw the light and were afraid, but they didn't understand the voice of him who spoke to me." (Act. 22:9)

This seems to be a contradiction in Gospel, but it is not. In Acts 22:9 it is said to sound like the words of a man (Paul) and it is not said that he was prophesying or filled with Holy Spirit. He was just mixed up in his direct speech. The Gospel is in no way contradictory.

"We are His witnesses of these things; and so also is the Holy Spirit, whom God has given to those who obey him." (Act. 5:32)

Isn't the Holy Spirit given to these who believe rather than these who obey?

"**... Did you receive the Spirit by the works of the law, or by hearing of faith?**" (Galatians 3:2)

In Acts 5:32 it did not say that Peter said this being filled with Holy Spirit, so these are human words and may be not true.

Heart (unconscious)

"Heart" in the Bible means unconscious (in a Freudian sense).

"**For out of the heart come forth evil thoughts, murders, adulteries, sexual sins, thefts, false testimony, and blasphemies.**" (Mt. 15:19)

"**For from within, out of the hearts of men, proceed evil thoughts, adulteries, sexual sins, murders, thefts, covetings, wickedness, deceit, lustful desires, an evil eye, blasphemy, pride, and foolishness. All these evil things come from within, and defile the man.**" (Mrk. 7:21-23)

"**The heart is deceitful above all things, and it is exceedingly corrupt: who can know it?**" (Jer. 17:9)

Some preachers preach "just follow your heart." While this may sound good, you are to follow God, not your heart.

"You have heard that it was said, 'You shall not commit adultery;' but I tell you that everyone who gazes at a woman to lust after her has committed adultery with her already in his heart." (Mt. 5:27-28)

This means that one who gazes at woman with lust is committing telepathic adultery with her in his mind unconsciously.

"Blessed are the pure in heart, For they shall see God." (Mt. 5:8)

"Heart" here refers to the unconscious part of a person. In this verse it means that to see God it is enough just to have pure subconsciousness, there doesn't seem to be any need for special psychic powers for this.

"… until the Lord comes, who will both bring to light the hidden things of darkness, and reveal the counsels of the hearts…" (1Cor. 4:5)

When Jesus comes back all of our unconscious thoughts will be revealed.

"For he is our peace, who made both one, and broke down the middle wall of partition. … that he might create in himself one new man of the two, making peace; and might reconcile them both in one body to God through the cross." (Eph. 2:14-16)

I assume this means that Christ merges both our conscious and our unconscious mind into one, removing the separation that exists.

Prayer

When we pray to God, should we want to be heard by angels, saints in heaven, etc.? The argument that we should want to be heard not just by God is that angels may hear our prayer and answer it. The argument that we should strive to be heard only by God is that our prayer should be to Him only and not be misdirected to other entities. Which of the two arguments bears the most weight? The correct answer is:

"But you, when you pray, enter into your inner chamber, and having shut your door, pray to your Father who is in secret, and your Father who sees in secret will reward you openly." (Mt. 6:6)

We should pray in secret, so that (as much as possible) we can only be heard by God.

Reverses of good and bad

"But many who are first will be last; and the last first." (Mrk. 10:31)

"Behold, there are some who are last who will be first, and there are some who are first who will be last." (Luk. 13:30)

Gospel tells us the following about the chief priests and elders in the church.

"the chief priests and the elders of the people came to him as he was teaching... Most assuredly I tell you that the tax collectors and the prostitutes are entering into the Kingdom of God before you." (Mt. 21:23-31) This means that the church priest and elders had a weaker faith in free salvation than corrupt thievish officials and prostitutes. They thought that salvation can be purchased using money (as in church funds), but salvation is free.

"**... but the free gift of God is eternal life in Christ Jesus our Lord**" (Romans 6:23) and is distributed according to the decision of God the Father.

"**No one can come to me unless the Father who sent me draws him, and I will raise him up in the last day**" (John 6:44), not by our money-filled crusades.

"**For, I think that God has displayed us, the apostles, last of all, like men sentenced to death...**" (1Cor. 4:9)

The Apostles will be the very last people in the Kingdom of Heaven, not the first as we may suppose.

"**... in humility, each counting others better than himself.**" (Phil. 2:3)

"Others" refer to unbelievers, while "himself" refers to believers. So believers should consider themselves below unbelievers. See more in my book "End of Gospel."

Chapter 11   Apocalypse

I am not a great expert on the Apocalypse, and I realize that there many books on this topic. However I will explain some Apocalyptic topics, including the Seven Trumpets that include a comet falling onto the Earth.

See my book "[End of Gospel](#)" to learn my opinion about whether the Apocalypse catastrophes can be canceled, and if we could enter into the kingdom of heaven without a war of heaven against mankind.

Falling comet

It appeared that the last Bible book, Revelation, contains not only spiritual but also a literal sense. Revelation chapter 8 describes the **catastrophe of the near future which is comparable only with a Great Diluvian**: A big comet which will fall onto the Earth and kill most of its inhabitants.

Whether the comet will fall before or after the Rapture of the Church is outside of the scope of my message.

Every word of this Bible fragment describes in details the catastrophe resulting from the falling comet. Unbelievers are not able to explain how the Author of Bible knows what will happen when a comet falls onto the Earth without having the scientific knowledge we have today. So let's proceed:

"When he opened the seventh seal, there was silence in heaven for about half an hour. I saw the seven angels who stand before God, and seven trumpets were given to them. Another angel came and stood over the altar, having a golden censor. Much incense was given to him, that he should add it to the prayers of all the saints on the golden altar which was before the throne." (Rev. 8:1-3)

As we will see from what comes after, this censor is without a doubt a comet. There will be much incense (i.e. smoke and dust), when the comet enters the atmosphere and strikes the ground.

The censor (comet) is golden. A great many riches in heaven will fall down to earth for greedy people to be sacrificed! I think pieces of gold and golden dust will be spread everywhere, reflecting the Sun. The altar is also golden, indicating there will be very rich churches in the day of God's punishment! Gold is one of the heaviest metals. Greedy men will have a very heavy punishment for their sins against God. The heavier the comet the more destruction it causes.

It is the big sacrifice to cleanse the Earth from any kind of evil. The world lies in evil and it will be cleansed one more time as it was at the time of the Diluvian.

By the way, is it not wonderful that in the New World (after the Second Coming of Christ) that gold will be used for street covering instead of asphalt.

The question arises, how and from where will a golden comet appear? One possible answer is that it is the result of a collision between a golden asteroid and a normal comet or another asteroid. (Yes, astronomers have found an asteroid made entirely of gold, it is a fact!)

"The smoke of the incense, with the prayers of the saints, went up before God out of the angel's hand." (Rev. 8:4)

The burst caused by the velocity of the comet's nucleus crashing to the Earth will be so great that part of the Earth's atmosphere will be ejected into outer space. As a result there will be less air on the Earth, making it more difficult to breathe.

Note that the comet is thrown by an angel in response to the prayers of the saints. This is not a random or an accidental catastrophe, but a planned attack by angels in direct response to people's sins.

"The angel took the censor, and he filled it with the fire of the altar, and threw it on the earth. There followed thunders, sounds, lightnings, and an earthquake." (Rev. 8:5)

This falling comet is fiery, becoming extremely hot as a result of friction in the atmosphere. Unlike most meteors that burn up in the atmosphere, this comet is large enough that it will remain intact. Due to the intense heat it will be a fiery mountain falling from the sky. The impact will result in a seismic shockwave, causing massive earthquakes all around the globe of such ferocity that many of the world's great cities will undoubtedly be leveled.

There will also be an awful thunder (heard on the entire Earth), and so many people will become deaf. There will be lightnings, firstly giant lightnings as the comet causes horrific atmospheric disruptions between the comet and the Earth during the short time it is falling. These primary lightnings will produce massive electromagnetic pulses while generating such powerful radio waves that they will cause anything metallic to sparkle even at a a great big distance from the point of impact. Many power lines and electronic devices will be destroyed by the electromagnetic sparkling. Additionally, the atmosphere affected by the comet will produce many great and large thunderstorms. During the time it is crashing down to earth, there will be also other sounds but they will be heard not by human ears; instead powerful radio waves will directly enter the skull and into the brain, sounding inside and letting people know immediately of the cataclysm that had just occurred. This will enable them to hear of the falling comet immediately without waiting for the sound of thunders to pass in the distance!

These were just the introductory passages. Now let us read the rest of the details:

"The seven angels who had the seven trumpets prepared themselves to sound. The first sounded, and there followed hail and fire, mixed with blood, and they were thrown to the earth. One third of the earth was burnt up, and one third of the trees were burnt up, and all green grass was burnt up." (Rev. 8:6-7)

Frequently a cloud of smaller objects of varying sizes will be found near comets. They appear when a comet's orbit nears the sun or a planet and the head is partially destroyed by gravity and the sun's heat. When the entire object enters the atmosphere these huge stones will fall to earth as fiery meteorites. Their velocity will be so intense it will seem as if a mass of cluster bombs has struck the earth. Upon impact they will be mixed with the blood of people and animals. The hot fragments will destroy and set on fire houses, cars, fields, anything it comes in contact with. The cosmic dust accompanying the comet will produce gigantic hailstones in the atmosphere. These hailstones, along with meteorites will kill millions and mix their blood. One third of the earth's surface will be a firestorm!

These burning meteorites will also ionize the stratosphere and destroy the ozone layer which protects us from the ultraviolet rays of the sun. If somebody were to go outside without special protective equipment they will become blind and develop skin cancer in a short time.

A large portion of the world's agriculture will be burned in the fires raging across the planet, but even worse will be the ultraviolet radiation that destroys all the green grass (including agricultural plants). So the next distress is massive amounts of famine, however there is no other country to turn to for help. Many people will kill each other and eat each other's flesh.

Because of the destruction of one third of the trees and all of the green grass, oxygen levels will begin to decrease making it even harder to breathe.

Satellites will be destroyed by the meteorite rain. This means there will be no means of communication such as the Internet, television or radio. In addition the power outages will mean not refrigeration and hospitals will be unable to provide proper care. Water will also become scarce due to not having power to run the pumping stations.

"The second angel sounded, and something like a great burning mountain was thrown into the sea. One third of the sea became blood, and one third of the living creatures which were in the sea died. One third of the ships were destroyed." (Rev. 8:8-9)

By now, for any reasonable Bible reader it should be obvious that Revelation 8 describes a falling comet exactly as it is described.

The events of Revelation 8:8 do not happen immediately after the preceding verse, but in the middle of the meteorite rain. The burning mountain is the comet's nucleus falling into one of the oceans. The words "big mountain" means that the nucleus will be comparable in size to Mt. Everest (8 km). The more the comet weight the greater the destruction. Previously I noted that the comet will be golden, but it is probably not as heavy as an 8 km piece of gold and is probably only partially golden.

The comet will breach a hole in the crust of the Earth, causing a new giant volcano to arise from the ocean. In the impact zone the water will become very heated because of the actual impact and the volcano.

In the region of the fall a large quantity of poisonous hydrogen sulfide will rise to the top of the ocean. Hydrogen sulfide is contained in both the lower levels of ocean water and at the bottom. Hydrogen sulfide is produced by certain kinds of bacteria. The poison, as well as the shock wave and increased temperature will kill life at the top levels living near the surface of the ocean and be replaced with bacteria which can live in with hydrogen sulfide. These bacteria are red and so the water will become red like blood. As a result, one third of the living animals in the ocean will die. Additionally the water will be stained red from the blood of the dead bodies of sea animals and fishes. The concentration of microorganisms in the water will be comparable to the concentration of cells in blood. In effect, water will become blood, just as the Bible says. Hydrogen sulfide is the substance which causes dead bodies to stink and bloat, so the very ocean will stink with the poison.

Super-tsunamis produced by the impact will destroy one third of the world's navies besides the ships destroyed by the meteorites. Also, although for some reason the Bible doesn't mention this, the tsunami's will destroy many on-shore cities, killing those that survived the earthquakes.

Airplanes are perfect targets to be destroyed by meteorites, and one-third of all the airplanes will be also destroyed. It will be impossible to flee to a secure place from the zone of the greatest destruction.

"**The third angel sounded, and a great star fell from the sky, burning like a torch, and it fell on one third of the rivers, and on the springs of the waters. The name of the star is called Wormwood. One third of the waters became wormwood. Many people died from the waters, because they were made bitter.**" (Rev. 8:10-11)

The meaning of these verses is less clear than the previous ones. Therefore I will only give a possible exegesis:

In 1985, a nuclear reactor in Chernobyl, Ukraine melted down releasing a massive dose of radiation. Interestingly, the word Chernobyl is translated as *wormwood*. Since the accident, the reactor has been buried in concrete known as Chernobyl's Sarcophagus to protect the world from the radiation that is still emanating from the reactor. In the years following the disaster the sarcophagus has become unstable and the concrete is beginning to crack. There is no guarantee that at some future date the sarcophagus will not collapse and release the radiation simmering inside.

Perhaps the passage in Revelation 8:10, 11 means that a splinter from the comet might strike the sarcophagus and destroy it. If this were to occur then the second Chernobyl catastrophe would be much worse than the first. The weather patterns would result in a great outburst of radioactive dust that will settle into the water table thus making nearly all of the water in Europe undrinkable, causing many to die. It is also possible that in addition to the radiation there are other toxic gases that have been building for decades, just waiting for the moment of its release. The Bible mentions that the water will have a noticeably bitter taste.

"The fourth angel sounded, and one third of the sun was struck, and one third of the moon, and one third of the stars; so that one third of them would be darkened, and the day wouldn't shine for one third of it, and the night in the same way." (Rev. 8:12)

Because of the vast amounts of cosmic dust accompanying the comet as it heats up, along with the smoke from the burned cities and forests, the atmosphere will become less transparent and the particulates will reflect back the sun's visible light rays. In fact the dust and smoke particles will become so dense that visibility will be reduced by one third.

Because of this, a long extremely cold winter will settle over the whole Earth. Everything will be frozen, killing most of the surviving people, plants and animals.

"I saw, and I heard an eagle, flying in mid heaven, saying with a loud voice, Woe! Woe! Woe for those who dwell on the earth, because of the other voices of the trumpets of the three angels, who are yet to sound!" (Rev. 8:13)

These verses say that the catastrophes which will soon follow will make what has just occurred seem tame by comparison. However, the following texts in this area are much harder to understand. Therefore, I now lay aside my exegesis.

Chapter 12   Further readings

I have not put into this book a commentary on Mt. 10:33; Mrk. 8:38; Luk. 9:26; Luk. 12:8-9 and some other verses. For information on them and many other interesting things see my other book "End of Gospel."

Now that you have read and seen some interesting examples of interpretations of the New Testament not found anywhere else, I would encourage you to visit my website about Old Testament: withoutvowels.org

Here you will learn a simple method of reading ancient Hebrew grammar without vowels. You will be amazed at how easy it is to read without having to follow the unnecessary rules about vowels. If you would desire, you are welcome to help me translate and interpret the entire Old Testament, as it was written without vowels, using the methods shown here. There is much work involved and your help would be welcome and needed.

If you don't want or have the time, or prefer not to work, I would still encourage you to please visit the site and read my commentary on Old Testament. While the information is not complete, what is there will open your eyes to yet more revelations from God's holy word.

This ebook is free. [Please donate to the author](#) and read "[End of Gospel](#)."

www.ingramcontent.com/pod-product-compliance
Lightning Source LLC
Chambersburg PA
CBHW051744230426
43670CB00012B/2158